Psychology and parenthood

Jean Gross

Open University Press
Milton Keynes · Philadelphia

Open University Press
12 Cofferidge Close
Stony Stratford
Milton Keynes MK11 1BY

and
242 Cherry Street
Philadelphia, PA 19106, USA

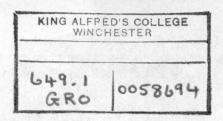
First published 1989

Copyright © Jean Gross 1989

British Library Cataloguing in Publication Data

Gross, Jean
    Psychology and parenthood.
    1. Parenthood. Psychological aspects
    I. Title
    155.6'46

    ISBN 0–335–09847–9
    ISBN 0–335–09846–0 Pbk

Library of Congress Cataloging-in-Publication Data

Gross, Jean.
    Psychology and Parenthood.
    Includes index.
    1. Parenting—Psychological aspects.
    2. Child rearing.
    I. Title.
HQ755.8.G755   1989   649'.1   88–31802

ISBN 0–335–09847–9
ISBN 0–335–09846–0 (pbk.)

Typeset by Scarborough Typesetting Services
Printed in Great Britain by
Biddles Ltd, Guildford and Kings Lynn

For Kate and Joanna

Contents

Preface

This book is the product of two different sets of experiences: those of being by profession a child psychologist, and those of being a parent. Through being a parent I learned which parts of the huge body of theory and research in child psychology are actually useful in coping with the day-to-day problems of bringing up children. It is a strong conviction that these useful parts do help, do matter, and should have a wider currency than that of academic textbooks, that prompted *Psychology and parenthood*.

In the pages that follow I have tried to stay close to the scientific evidence, and to base any suggestions on parenting techniques, or methods of handling particular problems, on proven effectiveness rather than supposition, pious hopes or any personal point of view. Nevertheless there will be academics who find the evidence incomplete, the conclusions open to dispute or the suggestions premature. I am sure they will often be right. This is, however, primarily a book for parents and professionals practising with children and their families, rather than a book for students of psychology. If it is to be useful, it must on occasion oversimplify complex and controversial issues. There must be much, too, that it omits.

By choice I have omitted to represent the knowledge we now have on the development of the child's linguistic and intellectual competence, on success and failure in school learning. There is much in this research that shows parents how they can best promote their child's intellectual growth, and which meets my criterion of 'usefulness'. But this is a topic in itself; I have restricted myself to the child's emotional and social development.

This book concerns parents, and children, of both sexes. When referring to the child I have used the pronoun 'he' and 'she' alternately, by chapter. For parents I have tried to use the he-or-she form to emphasize a belief that parenting and books on parenting are not just for or about mothers. The term 'parent' should be read as referring to whoever assumes a parenting role for a child: anyone from a grandfather to a paid nanny who cares for the child on the very intimate, personal and long-term basis which parenting implies.

Acknowledgements

The author and publishers are grateful to:

Pergamon Journals Ltd for permission to quote from the *Journal of Child Psychology and Psychiatry*, vol. 8, Patterson G. R., McNeal S., Hawkins N. and Phelps R. 'Reprogramming the social environment', © Pergamon Press Ltd., 1967.
National Society for Performance and Instruction for permission to quote from *National Society For Programmed Instruction Journal* vol. 4, no. 7, © National Society for Performance and Instruction, 1965.
Jossey-Bass for permission to quote from Shure M. and Spivak G. *Problem Solving Techniques in child-rearing* © Jossey-Bass, 1978.

1 Parenting: a two-way process

The direction of effect

There is a widespread assumption that children are as they are – good or naughty, aggressive or friendly, shy or sociable – largely because of the way their parents bring them up. This assumption is often strongest outside the family: neighbours, teachers and friends are quick to connect children's characteristics with the way they are treated at home. Parenting, in this way of thinking, is something that is done *to* children; children themselves are more or less passive recipients of their upbringing.

Within the family things may look different. Any parent of more than one child soon becomes aware that the same family background produces children who are very different from one another, that the individuality of their children forces them to react to each child in a unique and special way, and that what works for one won't work for all. Parents know that their children are not blank sheets on which they can write whatever message they choose. From the beginning, even from birth, children influence their parents' behaviour just as much as the parents influence them.

It took psychology some time to come around to this relatively obvious conclusion. At first psychological research concentrated solely on the possible effects on children of things parents do *to* them: breast or bottle feeding, timing and methods of toilet-training, types of discipline, separation from the mother. If a relationship was found – between, for example, the parents' use of physical punishment and aggressive behaviour in their children – the implied conclusion was always one-way: the children were more aggressive *because* they imitated or were frustrated by their parents' tendency to lash out. Then a possible set of alternatives was pointed out for this and many other findings[1] – that some parents are pushed into using

fairly strong disciplinary techniques (like physical punishment) by *the way
their children are*. An aggressive child may well also be assertive, overactive,
stubborn, hard to control, hard to live with, and easy to smack.

Psychological research is now much better at taking into account the
complex interactions between children's own temperamental characteristics
and the way their parents react to them. In a recent study, for example,
which found that depression in mothers was associated with behaviour
problems in their young children,[2] the possibility that mothers might
become depressed *because* their children are naughty or difficult is given as
much weight as the possibility that children react to their mothers'
depression and preoccupation with naughty and difficult behaviour.

This matters for parents because of the question of guilt. Every parent
worries about his or her child and has times when things do not seem to be
going well. Even with their knowledge of the child's individuality, it is easy
for parents to blame themselves and wonder where they went wrong. While
a major part of this book is devoted to the idea that parents can make use of
current psychological knowledge to alter and improve the way they relate to
their children, the best starting point for such alterations is a rational interest
in new ideas rather than the anxiety that stems from self-blame. If your
children are quarrelsome, untidy, restless or contrary (and whose aren't?),
there may be things you can do about it – but it is important to remind
yourself that they aren't necessarily this way because you made them so.
'How they are' is as important as 'how you are' in the parent–child equation.

Children as individuals

'How they are' includes many factors: children's age, sex, position in the
family. Boys, for example, may be harder in some respects to rear than girls:
even from birth they are more physically active than girls, from the
pre-school years onwards they are more aggressive, and more prone to most
types of learning and behaviour problems (boys outnumber girls, for
example, in a ratio of approximately 2 : 1 in their rate of maladjustment and
4 : 1 in reading difficulties). Boys receive more physical punishment than
girls, and parents play in a different way with their sons (more rough and
tumble play, and less verbal interaction) than with their daughters.[3] Parents'
reactions vary, too, depending on the birth order of their children: they
spend more time in affectionate social interaction with their first-borns,
whilst at the same time tending to be more anxious, pressurizing and
controlling. With the second child they are more relaxed, consistent and
confident although less involved.[4]

The most important individual differences that affect the way children
are handled are those of temperament. Even small babies, as every parent
knows, differ from each other in consistent ways in their early personalities.

A fascinating research project, called the New York Longitudinal Study, carried out by Thomas and Chess, has succeeded in identifying and quantifying the facets of early temperament.[5] Thomas and Chess outline nine such facets: activity level (how much babies move about during bathing, eating, playing, dressing, etc.), rhythmicity (how closely they stick to a predictable routine in times of sleeping, eating and elimination), approach–withdrawal (whether they generally like or dislike new experiences), adaptability (how soon they adapt to a new person, place, food or toy), intensity (ranging from a pattern of usually mild emotional responses like whimpering or smiling to intense responses such as loud crying or laughing), threshold (how strong a stimulus change, like a small difference in the temperature of food or a slightly wet nappy, would be enough to make them react), mood (happy, joyful behaviour as opposed to crying and miseries), attention–persistence (the length of time they will stick at a given activity) and distractability.

The New York researchers also found that some of these infant personality traits tended to cluster together. The most common pattern they found, which they labelled 'the easy child' consisted of high rhythmicity, positive mood, approach, high adaptability and low intensity. The exact opposite pattern, the 'difficult child', described babies who were irregular in their habits, generally disliked new experiences and were slow to adapt to them, and were usually in a strongly negative mood with much crying and fussing. These difficult children made up ten per cent of the sample studied. A third pattern was labelled 'slow to warm up' and was characterized by low activity, withdrawal, low adaptability, negative mood and low intensity. Both difficult and slow-to-warm-up children were harder for their parents to rear than the easy children; their temperamental differences had important implications for the way they were handled, and there were some long-term effects of those early differences. At the age of four and five years, some seventy per cent of the original 'difficult' infants were showing behaviour problems when Thomas and Chess followed them up, compared with eighteen per cent of the 'easy' babies.

To some degree events before and during birth, it is thought, can influence a child's temperament. We know, for example, that there is an association between a difficult birth, early irritable and fussy behaviour in the baby, and later sleep problems.[6] Another study confirmed the association between difficult births and later sleep problems, finding also that the children with difficult births were later more resistant to change, anxious on starting school, and generally more troublesome than a comparison group.[7]

Heredity, however, is probably more important in determining temperament. In all nine of Thomas and Chess's factors, pairs of identical twins (from a single split egg and with identical genetic blueprints) are more similar to each other than are pairs of fraternal twins (from two separate eggs and with a genetic blueprint no more similar than that of any two brothers and sisters).[8] In older children the same kind of twin studies have shown a substantial genetic component in sociability, emotionality and anxiety levels,[9] as well as in many diverse oddities of child behaviour which are commonly seen as in some way the parents' 'fault' – stammering, bedwetting, nail-biting and sleepwalking are examples.[10]

Children in charge

If children affect their upbringing indirectly, through 'the way they are', they also affect it very directly and simply in things that they *do*. From the moment of birth, they have an enormous amount of power over their parents. They can deliver large amounts of what psychologists might call 'aversive stimuli' if things are not to their liking; as babies they cry, as toddlers they whine or have tantrums, as they get older they learn to sulk and storm. They can also simply look downcast and sad. Parents find all such signs of discontent painful to watch; they have a very strong motivation to see their children happy and content. While certain types of discontent are painful only for the child's own parents (it is possible to be very unbothered by sulks or tantrums of other people's children), others are universally aversive. The cry of the human infant, for example, has been shown to be maximally pitched and varied so that it is both impossible to ignore or to get used to. Most adults will do a great deal (even get out of bed repeatedly in the small hours) if the child has taught them in the past that such behaviour will make the crying stop. Herein lies the child's power. The discovery of the extent of that power is one of the earliest and greatest shocks of parenthood.

Parents of older children, however, are often not aware of the power their children are still exercising. At the lower end of the scale, this power can take the form of minor pressures on parents – to go to the sweet shop more often than they want to, to buy one school coat rather than another less fashionable one, to let the carrots be left: all the conversations that begin with 'You can't' and end in 'Oh, all right then – if you must'. At the upper end of the scale we find the full-blown brat syndrome: children who make such good use of tantrums and threats that others feel totally helpless to control them. Such children are not at all uncommon and can serve as a warning of the potential dangers if the child, rather than the parents, ends up in charge. Here is a case study:

> Jeff, aged eight and a half, was referred to a child guidance clinic because he had frequent temper tantrums and physically attacked his mother, teachers and peers. His parents had tried spanking and withdrawing privileges, but with no success. Jeff was in charge of family activities, to the extent that he dictated, for instance, when his mother could and could not sit in the living room. In school he bullied and told tales and

needed constant attention from his teacher. He had no friends. He wet his bed every night and suffered from skin allergies and chronic asthma. He had always been a sickly child, from the time of his first asthma attack at sixteen months; various respiratory illnesses followed and the parents began to give in to his demands for fear of starting off or aggravating his illness. He was an only child.

Observation of the mother and Jeff together showed that she attended and spoke to him constantly in a meek, soft monotone which changed very little even when she was trying to correct him. Much of her behaviour seemed to be aimed at pacifying Jeff at all costs, and with good reason. If she refused, for example, to give him a snack, he would threaten to hit or bite her, scream or have an asthma attack and, if she still refused, he would carry out the threat. No expressions of warmth between Jeff and his mother could be noted in any of the observations. When asked how she felt about him, she stated that she did not like him and felt terrified by him.[11]

Poor Jeff, and poor mother. It was possible to help this family successfully, and the way in which this was done is discussed in chapter 6. At the moment it is important to note that what happened between Jeff and his parents could never be described in simple one-directional terms. From the beginning there was Jeff with a strong, dominant personality and his mother with an unassertive one. There were the accidents of his illness and his position as an only child. There were things his parents taught him to do (threaten and tantrum), and there were things he taught his parents to do (buy peace at a price). There was an interaction – a two-way process.

References

1 R. W. Bell, 'A reinterpretation of the direction of effects in studies of socialization', *Psychological Review*, 75 (1968), 81–95.

2 N. Richman, J. Stevenson and P. J. Graham, *Preschool to School: a Behavioural Study*, London, Academic Press, 1982.

3 E. E. Maccoby and C. N. Jacklin, 'Psychological sex differences', in M. Rutter (ed.), *Scientific Foundations of Developmental Psychiatry*, London, Heinemann Medical Books, 1980.

4 M. Rutter, *Maternal Deprivation Re-assessed*, 2nd edn., Harmondsworth, Penguin Books, 1981.

5 A. Thomas and S. Chess, *Temperament and Development*, New York, Brunner/ Mazel, 1977.

6 N. Blurton-Jones, M. C. R. Fereira, M. Farquar-Brown and L. Macdonald, 'The association between perinatal factors and later night-waking', *Develop. Med. Child Neurol.*, 20 (1978), 427–34.

7 L. E. Ucko, 'A comparative study of asphyxiated and non asphyxiated boys from birth to five years', *Develop. Med. Child Neurol.*, 7 (1965), 643–57.

8 A. M. Torgersen and E. Kringlen, 'Genetic aspects of temperamental differences in infants', *J. American Academy of Child Psychiatry*, 17 (1978), 433–44.
9 H. H. Goldsmith, 'Genetic influences on personality from infancy to adulthood,' *Child Dev.*, 54 (1983), 331–55.
10 H. Bakwin and M. Davidson, 'Constipation in twins', *Amer. J. Dis. Child*, 121 (1971), 179–81.
11 M. E. Bernal, J. S. Duryee, H. L. Pruett and B. J. Burns, 'Behaviour modification and the brat syndrome', *J. Consulting and Clinical Psychology*, 32 (1968), 447–55.

2 Parenting styles

It is because children are individuals, and what works with one does not necessarily work with another, that psychological research has found it particularly difficult to establish clear-cut relationships between parenting techniques and their effects on the child. Nevertheless some recent findings are beginning to allow a few broad generalizations to be made. These findings do suggest that most parents have a recognizable style of interacting with their children, a style which is consistent over time – though not necessarily between the two parents in any one family.[1] One such style, which was the subject of much early research, is variously labelled *overprotective* or *overindulgent*.[2,3] Other styles – *permissive, authoritarian* and *authoritative* – have been identified and described more recently.[4] In this chapter we will look at some of the fascinating studies of these four styles of parenting, and their relationships with the way children develop and behave.

The overprotective parent

The research on this parenting style has confined itself exclusively to mothers; we know little about overprotection in fathers. This kind of mother has a very loving, close relationship with the child. She hates to see the child unhappy and will go to great lengths to prevent this. The child is the most important person to her, the hub of family life, a precious possession. His wants and needs are put first, and his parents are at his beck and call. The parent does many things for the child that he can do for himself, babies him and waits on him long after the age at which this might be appropriate. There is far more contact between the mother and child – both physical and social – than is normal: one study,[3] for example, showed that nearly one third of overprotected children referred to a particular child guidance clinic (all over eight years of age) were still sleeping with their mothers. The mother exercises a very tight control over the child's life. She determines whom he plays with and where he plays. She tends to fight his battles for him and tells him to come to her for help in case of teasing or quarrels.

About the causes and the outcome of this style of parenting (we should say 'presumed outcome' since the direction of effects has not been unequivocably established) we know quite a lot. Sometimes in these families the child has been born after a long wait, the death of other children, complications in the pregnancy or a history of miscarriages. Sometimes he has had many illnesses or operations which make him seem vulnerable and particularly precious to the parents. Sometimes the parents themselves have been brought up in homes lacking warmth and love and want to make up to their child for all they lacked in their youth. Guilt, too – real or imagined – on the parents' part for something they are not doing for the child in one area can bring overindulgence in other areas. A poor relationship between the parents can push some mothers into an unduly close relationship with the child in order to make up for what is missing in the marriage.

Children brought up in this sort of atmosphere have been found to be passive, submissive and dependent. They are more likely than other children to be anxious and inhibited. The dangers of any type of indulgent parenting, even less extreme than that described above, seem to be that it leaves the child ill-prepared for an outside world that is less kind than the world at home. He may get a picture, too, of himself as helpless and immature and inferior, from the way his parents treat him, and he may spend the rest of his life living up to this helpless image. He may not learn the kind of 'I can cope' self-statement which appears to be important in preventing later anxieties. Indulgence, even when very well meant, deprives him of the chance to learn responsibility. He learns that he does not have to do things for himself – eventually someone else will always do them for him. He quickly learns that he does not have to remember for himself – someone else will remind him. A child who always 'forgets' usually has a mother who always remembers. A child who 'won't', at different stages of his development, feed himself with a spoon or do up his own shoe buckles or make his own bed usually has a parent who will. Parents of handicapped children often have to fight particularly hard against this very natural tendency to help the child out even beyond the time when he has outgrown the need for help: overprotection can be a real difficulty for them.

The permissive parent

The permissive parent shares with the overprotective parent a tendency to let the child have his own way but differs in placing few controls or restrictions on him. Permissiveness can take place in an emotional climate anywhere on the scale between warmth and coldness; permissiveness in a cold, rejecting climate would be called neglect, while permissiveness in a warm and loving home might be called indulgence. The children of neglecting parents are a sad and important group, more at risk for all kinds of antisocial behaviour problems as they grow up, and in particular for delinquency.[5] The consequences of rejection and neglect are fairly obvious to all of us, however, and need little elaboration. This section will concentrate on the more controversial effects of permissiveness in the climate of warm and responsible parenting.

One kind of permissive parent, a very middle-class phenomenon, is a familiar figure. He or she has lived through an era where many doctors and experts reacted against the prevailing climate of nineteenth-century attitudes – for example, that children should be seen and not heard, they should as infants be fed on schedule and not picked up when they cry. He or she has read Dr Spock and absorbed the message that children have feelings we should respect and needs we should meet without too much regard for rules and schedules. The child of this kind of permissive parent will as a baby have been picked up most times he cried. He will have been allowed to come into his parents' bed if he woke up lonely in the night. He will not have been weaned from bottle or breast at an early age. He will probably have toilet-trained himself when he was 'ready', perhaps at nearly three. His jealousy of younger brothers and sisters is understood and his aggression tolerated. He is allowed to choose how he spends his free time, and his parents are concerned not to force any of their attitudes – moral, religious or social – on him.

Another kind of permissiveness is described by Elizabeth and John Newson in the studies they have been carrying out for many years in the urban community of Nottingham.[6] They have looked at child-rearing in working-class families, where permissiveness takes other forms. They describe patterns where the child is allowed to play out in the street very much when and with whom he chooses, is expected to fight his own battles and look after himself. Set routines are few; the child might have no particular bedtime and fall asleep on the sofa when watching television in the late evening and then be carried up to bed, and he might help himself to a snack whenever he is hungry and eat it wherever he happens to be at the time, rather than sitting down with the family at formal mealtimes.

Permissive parenting of whatever type has, it seems, both positive and negative correlates in the child. Early research in the new era of freedom for children focused on the positive consequences of less strict homes (self-confidence, independence, initiative, spontaneity and creativity) and the negative effects of parental dominance and control. One study[7] concludes that firm strict adult control seems to produce the conforming, obedient child, handicapped in initiative and shy. It was also noted, however, that children from permissive homes were more aggressive and disobedient. Recent researchers[4,8,9] have repeated this aspect of the findings. They describe a child who tends to be impulsive, aggressive, low on self-control and intolerant of frustration. He is the three-year-old who goes out visiting and races around touching (perhaps breaking) everything in sight. Nursery-school staff may tell the parents they are a little worried about his relationships with other children. Later on, his teachers may comment on his poor concentration and lack of sustained effort. Again, he has to learn that society may have expectations of him which his parents do not have, that it makes demands on him which he is not used to, and often imposes the very frustrations from which his parents have tried hard to protect him.

There is another problem for him too. Some psychologists feel that children need what they call *limits* on their behaviour. A child is subject to some powerful emotions – rage, hate, jealousy. He needs, it is thought, external controls to help him manage these feelings. Without such controls the strength of his feelings can be very frightening to him: he genuinely fears what he might do, what harm he might cause. Much of a young child's naughty behaviour, in this theory, can be seen as a kind of testing out of the limits – a request for a kindly adult to make clear what is acceptable and what is not. If the adult feels unable to draw some firm lines to tell him just where to stop, he can become anxious and confused.

Authoritarian parents

The child of the authoritarian parent will, by contrast, be very sure where the lines are drawn. Authoritarian parents are the opposite in every respect of the permissive parent. They believe, often because this is how they themselves were brought up, that a parent's word is law and a child should always do as he is told. 'Because I say so' is their response when the child questions an edict. They do not believe in giving explanations or making allowances. To discipline the child they tend to use physical punishment, the threat of deprivation of material possessions or privileges; they may frighten the child into compliance by conjuring up bogeymen and warning him of the dire consequences of disobedience.

Psychologists have examined the presumed effects of authoritarian methods on the child's developing sense of right and wrong and on his level of aggression. The results suggest few positive benefits to the child and quite a lot of potential dangers.

A child who parents use only the power-assertion method of discipline described here tends to score low on a variety of measures of moral development, including resistance to temptation, experience of guilt after wrongdoing, altruism, honesty and helpfulness.[10] Children like this are dependent on the fear of being found out, and the threat of punishment, rather than on any internalized standards (conscience), to make them toe the line. In laboratory experiments they will not cheat in a game, for example, if an adult is in the room but they will cheat if the adult goes out. They are likely to have low self-esteem[11] and may be miserable and withdrawn.[4] If they receive a great deal of physical punishment they are likely to be more aggressive than other children; as we have seen, the direction of effect here is not altogether clear, but the finding that the parents' use of physical punishment *early* in his life can predict how aggressive the child will be *later on*[12] suggests that the link may be causal.

The authoritative parent

This kind of parent also sets firm limits for the child and believes in the importance of rules and routines – fixed bedtimes, family mealtimes, respect for the rights, property and feelings of others, constructive use of free time, intolerance of aggression in any form. The methods of enforcing the rules, however, are very different. He or she may use physical punishment occasionally – a quick smack rather than a real hiding – but will always want to explain to the child in words where he went wrong. In particular, this parent tries to make the child aware of the consequence of his actions for others. When the child does as he is told, the parents show immediate pleasure. They spend quite a lot of time playing with the child; the relationship is warm and close, but without the dependency which characterizes the overindulged child's dealings with his parents. The child is encouraged to take responsibility and do things for himself. His parents are willing to listen to his reasonable demands and let him take a share in family decision-making. Ultimately, however, they and not the child are in charge of the outcome.

This parenting style relates to compliant, well-behaved children with a highly developed sense of right and wrong. They have high self-esteem,[13] are good at resisting temptation, quick to accept blame, capable of altruism and self-sacrifice. They are rarely aggressive; outsiders see them as self-reliant and self-controlled. Teachers like them a lot, and so do other children. On the negative side, some researchers[7] interpret their personality pattern as docile and overconforming. Before we accept authoritative parenting as an ideal – which is the implication of many recent reviews of child-rearing practices[14,15] – more research would be useful, particularly perhaps to discover whether children brought up in this way become overly conscience ridden, too quick to blame themselves and feel at fault, burdened by guilt for trivial wrongdoings, so eager to please that they are afraid to say no. The take-up of courses on self-assertiveness by many well-brought-up adults suggests that even an apparently ideal child-rearing pattern may have subjective drawbacks, though these have not yet been systematically explored.

References

1 E. E. Maccoby and J. A. Martin, 'Socialization in the context of the family: parent–child interaction', in E. M. Hetherington (ed.) *Socialization, Personality and Social Development*, vol. IV, *Handbook of Child Psychology*, 4th edn., New York, Wiley, 1983.
2 L. E. Hewitt and R. L. Jenkins, *Fundamental Patterns of Maladjustment: The Dynamics of their Origin*, Springfield, Illinois, 1949.
3 D. M. Levy, *Maternal Overprotection*, New York, Columbia University Press, 1943.
4 D. Baumrind, 'Current patterns of parental authority', *Develop. Psych. Monogr.*, 4, 1, Pt. 2 (1971).
5 W. McCord and J. McCord, *Origins of Crime*, New York, Columbia University Press, 1959.
6 J. Newson and E. Newson, *Four Years Old in an Urban Community*, London, Allen and Unwin, 1968.
7 G. Watson, 'Personality differences in children related to permissive parental discipline', *J. Psychol.*, 44 (1957), 227–49.
8 M. R. Yarrow, J. D. Campbell and R. V. Burton, *Child Rearing: An Inquiry into Research and Methods*, San Francisco, Jossey-Bass, 1968.
9 D. Olweus, 'Familial and temperamental determinants of aggressive behaviour in adolescent boys: a causal analysis', *Develop. Psychol.*, 16 (1980), 644–60.
10 M. L. Hoffman, 'Empathy, role-taking, guilt and development of altruistic motives', in T. Lickona (ed.), *Moral Development and Behaviour*, New York, Holt, Rinehart and Winston, 1976.
11 S. Coopersmith, *The Antecedents of Self-Esteem*, San Francisco, Freeman, 1967.
12 D. Farrington, 'The family background of aggressive youths', in L. Hersov, M. Berger, D. Schaffer (eds), *Aggression and Antisocial Behaviour in Childhood and Adolescence*, Oxford, Pergamon, 1978.
13 M. L. C. Comstock, 'Effects of perceived parental behaviour on self-esteem and adjustment', *Dissertation Abstracts*, 34, 465B, 1973.
14 M. Rutter and A. Cox, 'Other family influences', in M. Rutter and L. Hersov (eds), *Child and Adolescent Psychiatry: Modern Approaches*, 2nd edn., Oxford, Blackwell Scientific Publications, 1985.
15 R. A. Hinde, 'Family influences', in M. Rutter (ed.), *Scientific Foundations of Developmental Psychiatry*, London, Heinemann, 1980.

3 The unsuccessful parent

Conclusions about desirable styles of parenting will probably always be controversial. There is more agreement, however, about styles that are undesirable – about the things that do *not* work than about those that do. This chapter is about the detailed analysis that some psychologists, notably Gerald Patterson in the USA,[1] have made of ineffective parenting. It is a chapter largely about 'how not to' parent.

Patterson and his co-workers have made a special study over many years of the aggressive, antisocial child: the child who is the despair of his teachers and the terror of the neighbourhood. Over two hundred and fifty such children and their families, referred to the Oregon Social Learning Centre, make up his clinical sample. Several hundred families with normal children were used as a comparison group. Observers sat in on everyday family interactions in the child's home, minutely coding the exact events that made up those interactions – a minimum of six observation sessions in each home, each session providing over twelve hundred such events to be analysed.

This exhaustive research, and that of others,[2,3] allows several features of unsuccessful parenting to be identified. We will look at each of them in turn.

Lack of rules

The parents of difficult, hard-to-manage children tend not to give explicit guidance on what they expect: in Patterson's terminology, there is a lack of 'house rules'. The child does not know what he is allowed to do and what he is not allowed to do, or for which behaviour he will be punished. The children might not, for example, consistently be expected to be home at set times, to finish homework, or help out in certain household chores.

Vague commands

The parents issue many more commands to their children than comparison parents, but the commands are vague. 'Why can't you be more tidy' would be more likely than 'pick up those toys'. There is a constant stream of irritable criticism, of 'nattering and nagging'. Instead of sticking to a few really important rules, and making sure these are adhered to, the parents comment on all sorts of things the child does, whether or not they really intend to stop him doing them. Instead of a few major confrontations there are many minor ones.

That this really is a causal relationship – in that nattering and nagging precedes bad behaviour rather than following it – is suggested by the finding in one experiment that parents of normal children can very easily make them behave badly, by increasing the number of commands they give.[4] Further support for the causal relationship (and this applies to Patterson's other features of unsuccessful parenting too) comes from the evidence that, if parents can be taught how to make clear rules and reduce their irritable nagging, the children's behaviour shows an instant improvement as a result.

Bad timing

Not from Patterson's work but from other American experiments[5] comes the suggestion that poorly timed commands are as important in leading to confrontation as are vague, too frequent ones. It has been shown that instructions to children (to change what they are doing) that come out of the blue and without warning are often unsuccessful. The young child will, for example, make less fuss on leaving a friend's house or a playground, or stopping an activity he is enjoying, if he is told *beforehand*: 'You have five minutes more, and then we must stop/leave.'

Conveying dislike for the child

The irritable nagging and shouting that characterizes unsuccessful parents conveys a general message of dislike for the child as a person, rather than specific criticism of things that he *does*. Children can respond constructively to requests to stop doing something in particular, but running them down in generalized critical ways is thought to produce low self-esteem and poor adjustment.[6] 'That was a silly thing to do' can be helpful, 'You stupid child' is not.

Empty threats

One of the clearest signs of ineffective parenting, in Patterson's studies, was a failure to follow through on commands and instructions. The parent may say, for example, 'Stop that!' 'Get down off there!' 'Give it back to her!' (often with an added threat '. . . or else . . .'), but if the child does not comply he or she *does nothing about it*. The child learns that many of his parents' threats are empty, while – like Jeff in chapter 1 – making sure to carry out his own implicit or explicit threats about what *he* will do if he does not get his own way. Very often, moreover, a child who is naughty is unclear about whether his parents are really angry and do mean him to stop what he is doing. During the treatment of Jeff, when his mother was instructed in how to be more forceful (tone of voice, facial expression) when telling him off, he asked 'Are you angry?': her expressed anger was clearly novel and surprising to him.

Ignoring good behaviour

Parents of Patterson's clinical sample failed to make an adequate differentiation between praise for good behaviour and punishment for bad. When their children did behave well, nobody told them so, so that they had even less chance (against the background of irritable nattering) to find out what they really were supposed to do. Changing this aspect of the parents' behaviour formed an important part of successful treatment for these families.

Lack of enjoyable shared activities

Patterson found that his families tended to have less social interactions and shared activities than others. There are studies, too, that show how one predictor of the likelihood a child will do as he is told is the amount the mother has played with the child in the past.[7] A major London research project on parenting[2] in mothers who themselves had been raised in children's homes and who had difficulties in coping (particularly with their first child) found differences in the way these mothers played with their children – not this time in overall amount of joint play, but in the way that they often ignored the child when he was trying to show his mother something or share with her his interest and excitement in a new discovery. Listening to children, joining in some of their play, and later joint interests and outings as a family clearly provide the foundation for effective parenting.

A background of marital discord

Marital discord has repeatedly been shown to be associated with behaviour problems in children;[8] this is the single factor on which every research project on antisocial conduct and delinquency agrees. Discord is the background, it appears, against which effective parenting is near impossible. Witnessing or, worse, becoming involved in parents' quarrels is unquestionably damaging to children, and parents preoccupied with their marital problems are not able to guide their children in a coherent way. Family disharmony is more important even than whether or not the family is intact: 'children from broken homes tend to function *better* than children from unhappy unbroken ones'.[9] The relationship between parents may be much harder to change than their styles of discipline, but the evidence is that, of all the things parents can do for their children, an attempt to resolve marital problems is likely to be the most worthwhile.

Conclusions

Strictly speaking, it would be premature to draw any conclusions about effective parenting from the results of research on ineffective families. Because parents who are having problems with their children fail to make clear house rules for them does not *necessarily* imply that effective parents do make rules. There is, however, evidence from some studies of particularly well-adjusted children and those with high self-esteem[7,10] that at least some of the factors Patterson has identified – particularly consistency in setting and enforcing limits – are as important by their presence as by their absence. We can, then, make a tentative list of guidelines for good parenting, which would run as follows:

1 Make rules for children on important issues, and make clear what those rules are. Certain rules can be seen as universal: not damaging or taking others' property, not hurting others physically, not causing danger to self or others by playing with matches, running on ahead in a busy street and so on. Other rules will vary from family to family: it is only worth specifying bedtimes, for example, if it really matters to you to have the children in bed promptly at a certain hour.
2 Give clear and simple instructions on the issues that really matter to you (where there are rules) but avoid 'nattering and nagging' about issues of less importance. The point is that if having the children in bed on time does *not* matter to you a great deal, and there is not a house rule on bedtime, then it is important not to turn on the children at ten o'clock one day and eight o'clock the next and berate them for not being in bed when you suddenly find their noise unbearable.
3 If an instruction is issued, it should always be followed through. If you don't intend to follow through, don't issue the instruction and risk losing your credibility.
4 If you do not like what the child is doing, make that clear without devaluing his personality; avoid labels like 'lazy', 'stupid', 'hateful',

'thoughtless' applied to the child. Apply them instead to his acts: 'You hit Jane, that was a very unkind thing to do.'

5 Make sure your signals, both of anger and pleasure, are emphatic and unmistakable. The child should know when you mean business; many children don't.

6 Let the child know when you do like what he is doing: 'You and Jane have played all afternoon *without* fighting – well done.' This kind of attention for positive behaviour is not part of most parents' everyday repertoire and does not come easily. It can, however, be learned, and is an indispensable tool for effective parenting. It is discussed in greater detail in the next chapter.

References

1 G. R. Patterson, *Coercive Family Process*, Eugene, Oregon, Castalia, 1982.
2 L. Dowdney, D. Skuse, M. Rutter, D. Quinton and D. Mrazek, 'The nature and qualities of parenting provided by women raised in institutions', *J. Child Psychol. Psychiatry*, 26 (1985), 599–625.
3 S. Peed, M. W. Roberts and R. Forehand, 'Evaluation of the effectiveness of a standardized parent training programme in altering the interaction of mothers and their noncompliant children', *Behav. Mod.*, 1 (1977), 223–50.
4 W. C. Lobitz and S. M. Johnson, 'Normal versus deviant children: a multimethod comparison', *J. Abnorm. Child Psychol.*, 3 (1975), 353–74.
5 H. R. Schaffer and C. K. Crook, 'Maternal control techniques in a directed play situation', *Child Dev.*, 50 (1979), 989–96.
6 D. Lewis, *You Can Teach Your Child Intelligence*, London, Sphere, 1983.
7 H. Lytton and W. Zwirner, 'Compliance and its controlling stimuli observed in a natural setting', *Dev. Psychol.*, 11 (1975), 769–79.
8 M. Rutter, *Maternal Deprivation Re-assessed*, 2nd edn., Harmondsworth, Penguin Books, 1981.
9 R. A. Hinde, 'Family influences', in M. Rutter (ed.), *Scientific Foundations of Developmental Psychiatry*, London, Heinemann, 1980.
10 S. Coopersmith, *The Antecedents of Self-Esteem*, San Francisco, Freeman, 1967.

4 Positive reward systems

The idea of using rewards for good behaviour as an everyday part of family life seems strange, uncomfortable and somehow immoral to many parents. Yet of all the practical applications of psychological research, it is the one which has been most useful to professionals who work with children's problem behaviour. It is also one which is increasingly finding its way into the lives of ordinary families. In this chapter we will look at the theory behind using rewards, positive consequences, or – in psychological jargon – 'positive reinforcement', to help children behave as we want them to.

Why use rewards?

Philip, aged seven, would not get himself ready for school in the morning. His mother would have to go into his room every few minutes to remind, scold and eventually shake him. This situation had been going on for several months, with no sign of improvement. Philip's mother decided to change her tactics. She was advised to ask him only once to get dressed, and to *stop* any nagging or criticizing. If Philip was not dressed within ten minutes, she was to go quietly in, hand him his clothes one by one and help him get dressed while praising enthusiastically any attempt to do part of the job himself. On each successive morning she was to repeat this, fading out her help and continuing to praise Philip for dressing himself. When he had managed without any help, she sent him to his father who also praised him warmly for 'being so grown up'; she also told Philip that because he had dressed himself quickly she would cook him bacon and egg that morning for a special treat. Within a week Philip was coming into his parents' room fully dressed and ready for school, before they were up.

In learning to get himself ready without fuss in the morning, Philip was following a basic principle of human behaviour – that *if what we do is followed by positive or pleasant consequences, we will be more likely to do it again in the future*. When he dressed himself, nice things happened, and so he began to dress himself more quickly and more often.

Why then did it not occur to his parents earlier that they should reward him for being good, rather than scold him for being bad? The answer seems to be that on the whole none of us find it easy to make use of the positive-consequences principle in our dealings with other people. Not only parents, but teachers, schools and many other social organizations have been shown to make very little use of attention or praise for *positive* behaviour – the behaviour they do want. Instead they focus on paying attention to the behaviour they *don't* want. The executive criticizes the secretary for slowness or typing errors but usually omits to say thank you for a fast and perfect piece of work. Teachers are found to attend to inappropriate behaviour in their classes three times more often than they do to appropriate behaviour.[1] Parents praise their children ('Well done', 'That's a good girl') relatively rarely in relation to other kinds of comment.[2] Most parents will recognize in themselves a tendency to stay *away* from the child and leave her on her own while she is playing quietly and happily, only intervening when things go wrong. Good behaviour is taken for granted, bad behaviour is instantly noticed.

Yet it is possible to redress this attention balance and provide more rewards for positive, desirable behaviour. Research in families, in schools and in other social settings has demonstrated this over and over again. Certificates for good school attendance do more to reduce truancy than prosecuting truants. Healthy eating habits show an immediate jump if children are given smiling-face stickers to put on a personal chart whenever they choose salad over chips or fresh fruit over ice-cream. Productivity increases if managers show appreciation of extra effort in the workforce. Children in their thousands have been helped to conquer fears, become less aggressive, become less hyperactive, become less dependent, stop stealing, stop bedwetting, stop bullying: all using positive reward systems. In practice, positive reward systems work.

Ethics

The first objection that many parents might make to the idea of using positive reward systems stems from an objection to the idea of manipulating the behaviour of others. The reply must be that whether they like it or not, they are already engaged in shaping their children's behaviour and have been from the day the child was born. There is a statistic from a recent observational study of normal children[3] which illustrates the extent of the shaping: parents were found to attempt to change their two-year-olds' behaviour against the child's will on average every *six* minutes. Two years is probably the peak age for such confrontations (rising again at adolescence?) but the disparities between what a child wants to do and what her parents want her to do are evident in any household, at any hour, on any day. If positive reward systems are used to promote behaviours in the child which help her to learn to accommodate to the needs of others, to function effectively in the family, with friends and at school, there can be no possible moral objection to their use. Nor does another possible objection, that of 'bribery', stand up to scrutiny: in our society when individuals are rewarded for desirable behaviour, the name it goes by is approval, praise, commission, salary – not bribery. Bribery refers to being paid off for undesirable behaviour.

What is a reward?

In some intriguing research, adults were asked to speak on a subject of their choice to a listener, who was primed at a certain point to begin nodding his head, smiling, making eye contact and approving noises whenever he heard a plural noun or whenever the speaker hesitated. The number of plurals and hesitations were recorded: they increased dramatically as a result of the change in the listener's behaviour.[1]

In another study tape recordings were made of the sounds made by small babies. If an adult smiled and briefly touched the baby every time it made a sound, it would make many more sounds than it had when there was no adult reaction.[5]

Jane was a six-year-old girl who had poor concentration and fine-muscle control. She disliked all games involving eye–hand co-ordination – writing, drawing, puzzles – and spent little time on them. Her mother had tried to encourage these activities at home, providing a desk and attractive drawing materials and manipulative toys. Jane remained uninterested. It was suggested to the mother that she go up to and talk to her daughter on every occasion when she did go to her desk, but to stay at a distance when she was playing other games. After several days of this, Jane was observed to be colouring, drawing and playing with the special toys for three-quarters of her time on average, compared to the almost zero manipulative play she had shown before.[6]

These examples show how attention, in almost any form, can act as an effective reward for behaviour: rewards are not just praise or presents. Even *negative* attention, attention which we might consider highly unpleasant, can act as a reward for behaviour. Philip, in the earlier example, became slower and slower in getting dressed as a result of his mother's daily scoldings. The rewarding effects of negative attention have been demonstrated in many studies in school classrooms and in the home:

> Ten children, six to ten years old, were observed in five classrooms. The children showed a variety of troublesome behaviours, disturbing others, disruptive noise, not getting on with their work. Their teachers, who were constantly reprimanding them, were asked to change their approach and to ignore all bad behaviour (unless one child was being hurt by another), while praising the children for behaviours compatible with learning: 'I like the way you're working quietly', That's the way I like to see you sit', 'I wish everyone was working like John'. Following this intervention, disruptive behaviour decreased by fifty per cent, shooting up again when the teachers were instructed to resort to their normal procedures.[7]
>
> A group of teenage boys were giving trouble around the pool (billiard) table in a social centre: scuffling, throwing the balls at each other and arguing. In the first phase of the experiment if a boy misbehaved he was immediately removed from the billiard room; this proved a successful technique. The purpose of the second phase was to observe the effects of verbal reprimand. When the boys misbehaved they were told 'I'm warning you' or 'Now cut it out' or 'Don't let it happen again'. Misbehaviour increased very rapidly indeed.

Once-in-a-while rewards

Another surprising finding from psychological research has been that once-in-a-while rewards can have *more* powerful effects on behaviour than more frequent rewards. This was originally demonstrated in laboratory experiments with animals:[8] experiments, for example, where rats learned to press one bar rather than another, or find their way through mazes, with different systems of reward. For new learning it worked best to give a reward to the desired behaviour one hundred per cent of the time. But rewards which came just once in a while were the best way of *keeping a learned behaviour going*. A rat who has received a pellet of food just once out of twenty times he has pressed a bar will go on pressing for much longer after pellets cease to appear than a rat who has had a pellet every time he pressed: clearly the first rat finds it easier to keep on hoping. So it is with dogs, monkeys, pigeons – and people.

A tool for understanding

The idea that positive consequences, particularly once-in-a-while positive consequences, increase the probability of a behaviour, and that attention in any form can act as a reward, is a tool all parents can use to help them understand what is going on between them and their children. Asking him or herself the following questions is a useful exercise for any parent:

● Have I taught my child to whine by paying attention to whining, trying to find out what the problem is and solve it for her?
● Have I taught my child to need a lot of attention (to appear with a book to read together whenever I sit down, to refuse to play happily unless I join in the game) by reading to her and playing with her whenever she asks?
● Have I taught her to have frequent tantrums by giving in if she does?
● Have I taught her not to listen to me because if she does listen and do as I say, nothing happens (no positive consequences), whereas if she doesn't she gets her own way and a lot of attention too?
● Has my child taught me to say everything twice, by doing as I ask (a positive consequence) at the second asking? or to nag, by doing it only after many askings?
● Has she taught me to be a kind, sympathetic, and attentive parent by stopping whining (another positive consequence) when I try to sort out all her difficulties?
● Has she taught me to spend every mealtime coaxing or nagging at her to eat up her food by *once in a while* consenting to clear her plate?

A tool for change

Having understood how positive consequences might be affecting what goes on between a parent and a child, it is often possible to make changes by altering the balance of rewards. There are, however, ways of using positive reward systems which work, and ways which do not. A parent contemplating using such a system needs to be aware of the following basic principles:

1 The behaviour to be reinforced must be clearly and precisely defined in such a way that the child, you or any other observer could always agree on whether or not that behaviour had been shown.

   Parents commonly promise their children treats if they are 'good' (CHILD: Can I stay up late to watch. . . ?. PARENT: Yes, if you're good.). This leaves the child with no clear idea about what she is expected to do, or not to do, in order to earn the reward. 'When you've managed not to argue with your sister for one whole day you can stay up late to watch . . .' would be more helpful. Another example might be a parent wishing a child to be more polite: he or she needs to ask what exactly is meant by politeness – is it eating with your mouth closed? Saying please and thank you? Not pushing past other people? This kind of thought has to be given to any words we might use in asking change of a child.

2 The three Cs. Reinforcement must be given clearly, contingently and at first continuously for the desired behaviour.

Being *clear* implies making your praise as warm, genuine and emphatic as you possibly can. It is no use at all to tell your child casually that she has been a good girl today. You have to tell her exactly what it was she did right this time, and you have to inject more pleasure into your voice and manner than you might feel the situation deserves. What the parent should aim at is the kind of reaction we give when our children take their first strokes at swimming or bring home a good school report. This sort of enthusiasm takes energy – but so does nagging.

Being *contingent* means that the reinforcement must come immediately after the desired behaviour. If you wait, you risk inadvertently rewarding whatever else the child has been doing in between. Reinforcing *continuously* means rewarding every instance of the desired behaviour to start with. This too is hard work, but fortunately it does not have to go on for very long. A few days of praising the child whenever she says 'excuse me' are followed by another week of praising her on some occasions and not on others – and then by praising her just once in a while ('That *was* polite'). In theory, this gradual reduction in reward might sound difficult. In practice, it is very easy, since it matches the natural tendency of the parent when trying something new to remember at the beginning to use it all the time, then to lapse more and more often. The only unnatural part of the process is remembering at the end to keep using the new technique occasionally rather than letting it lapse altogether – in other words, not taking the child's good behaviour for granted. Philip's parents, in the example on dressing for school, would still need to show pleasure on occasion ('Dressed already – oh that is nice').

3 The last principle of positive reward systems concerns *shaping*: that is, evoking a desired behaviour by rewarding approximations to that behaviour. It frequently happens that the behaviour a parent wants to see never happens, and so cannot be rewarded. Philip, for example, did not dress himself. In these cases it is necessary at first to reward small steps towards the final goal; to praise Philip one day for pushing his arm into the sleeve his mother holds out, to praise him the next for pushing both arms in, the next for putting his arms in the sleeves without her holding them out . . . and so on. Shaping is an extraordinarily powerful tool, which has again been extensively investigated in the psychological laboratory. A particularly compelling example of its use comes from the work of Lovaas[9] and his associates in teaching mute autistic children to speak. These children were at first rewarded merely for looking at their teacher. After they had learned to attend in this way, they were rewarded for making any sort of sound. When they were making many sounds, they were rewarded only if they made a sound immediately after the teacher made one, and

later only for successively closer approximations to the teacher's sound. From imitating sounds the training went on to words, phrases and eventually sentences.

An illustration

An illustration of how shaping (and the other principles we have looked at) can contribute to the growth of *un*desirable behaviour comes from this analysis, by Homme and Tosti,[10] of whining behaviour in children:

> The behaviour wanted is whining. Therefore, one ought to wait till a little whining occurred, then reinforce. For the reinforcer, attention alone will do. If one wants to administer a better-than-average reinforcer, he would make the attention emotional. Scream at the child 'Will you stop that whining!!' If that is too much trouble and one still wants whining strongly reinforced, something else can be found to add to attention. Ice cream, soda pop, candy . . . should do it. Note that the rule about reinforcing a first approximation has been obeyed. Any sort of whine will do for the first trial. Even an inadequate whine will do at first. Next time reinforcement will be withheld until the whining gets a little louder. The time after that the whining must be still louder before it is reinforced. One can anticipate . . . that whining will soon be strong and loud. Further, not every response has been reinforced – only occasional ones. This means that whining will be extremely difficult to get rid of . . . There you have it. Through the reinforcement of successive approximations, you have shaped up, theoretically, a strong, persistent whining response. Theoretically?

A summary

Summing up the principles of reinforcement as a parent might use them, we can see that he or she needs first to identify very precisely something the child should do more of, then cease to ignore it when it does occur and begin instead to praise or otherwise reward the child clearly and immediately on every occasion that she does it, or something close to it. In the next chapter we will look more closely at how to put these basic principles into practice.

References

1 H. Walker and N. Buckley, 'Teacher attention to appropriate and inappropriate classroom behaviour', unpublished manuscript, CORBEH, Department of Special Education, University of Oregon, 1971.
2 L. Dowdney, D. Skuse, M. Rutter and D. Quinton, 'The nature and qualities of parenting provided by women raised in institutions', *J. Child Psychol. Psychiatry*, 26 (1985), 599–625.

3 C. Minton, J. Kagan and J. Levine, 'Maternal control and obedience in the two-year-old', *Child Dev.*, 42 (1971), 1873–94.
4 M. Argyle, *Social Interaction*, London, Methuen, 1969.
5 Y. Brackbill, 'Extinction of smiling responses in infants as a function of reinforcement schedule', *Child Dev.*, 29 (1958), 115–24.
6 R. Vance-Hall and M. Broden, 'Behaviour changes in brain-injured children through social reinforcement', *J. Exptal. Child Psychol.*, 5 (1967), 463–79.
7 W. C. Becker, C. H. Madsen, C. R. Arnold and D. R. Thomas, 'The contingent use of teacher attention and praise in reducing classroom behaviour problems', *J. Special Education*, 1 (1967), 287–307.
8 B. F. Skinner, *Science and Human Behaviour*, New York, MacMillan, 1953.
9 O. I. Lovaas, 'A programme for the establishment of speech in psychotic children', in J. K. Wing (ed.), *Early Childhood Autism*, New York, Pergamon, 1966.
10 L. E. Homme and D. T. Tosti, 'Contingency management and motivation', *National Society for Programmed Instruction Journal*, 4 (1965), no. 7.

5 Reward systems in practice

Any behaviour can be increased by rewarding it, but in practice parents find reinforcement systems most useful for the kinds of behaviour which always seem to lead to nagging. Many parents find they spend more time than they wish in issuing their children with nagging negatives: don't do this, stop doing that, for goodness sake why can't you . . ., I've told you a hundred times not to . . . It is helpful to focus on the situations that prompt such negatives and make them (one at a time) the target of positive reward systems – from tidiness to table manners, from the child doing his violin/recorder/piano practice to his wiping his feet when he comes in from outside. The examples may seem trivial, but any parent knows that it is an accumulation of issues like these that can turn the home into a family battleground and damage the quality of his or her relationship with the child. If it proves difficult to identify the issues that are causing problems, and the parent is only aware of the child's general awfulness, he or she can:

- Keep a diary for a few days, in which is recorded a blow-by-blow account of family interactions.
- Answer the question 'In what three ways would you like your child to be different?', making sure to break down each answer into observable behaviours: 'I wish he wouldn't hit his brother; I wish he wouldn't get into fights in the playground; I wish he wouldn't shout at me.'

Whom to reward

To avoid complaints by other children in the family that they are being left out of reward systems, it is often easier to devise simultaneous systems for everyone. The behaviour of one child may be the main focus of your concern at any particular time, but it will always be possible to find something for a brother or sister to work on too. If Mary is being rewarded for getting her homework done promptly, then her small sister can also have a star chart (see p. 28) for helping to pick up her toys at tidy-up time. Some of the most useful reward systems are those you can use with *all* your children: for example, cultivating a habit of not responding to them when they complain over trivial grievances, while praising them all warmly for 'not moaning' on long walks, tedious shopping trips and after minor hurts.

How to reward

The first and simplest rewards to try out are social: praise, smiles, hugs and, for young children, picking them up, singing to them, tickling, rough and tumble – whatever they enjoy. Using social rewards like these is not as easy as it sounds. Most parents comment that it feels artificial, and they feel silly, if they go up to their children, for example, when they are not quarrelling, and say 'You two *are* playing nicely, I'm so pleased.' And yet it can be done: many of us are quite comfortable when shaping boys out of expressing strong emotions ('Brave boy, you're not crying').

Over time, it does become less artificial; to begin with, parents can teach themselves to be better reinforcers by setting aside a half-hour period each day when they look at the clock every five minutes and then go and say something nice to another family member: wife, husband or child. Such a deliberate attempt at change is particularly needed in any of us who recognize in ourselves the tendency to become what Gerald Patterson calls 'a contemporary Xanthippe':

> Even our limited experience in making observations in the homes of families being treated suggests the ubiquitous presence of a syndrome of maternal behaviour which we have labelled as 'Xanthippe'. This woman seems to use aversive techniques to control the behaviour of most of the people in her immediate environment, including my observers. She seldom, if ever, attends to the occurrence of socially adaptive behaviour in her child, and when she does, states 'that is what he ought to do, why should I reward him for that?' The 'lack of attending' and 'lack of rewarding' make her a very unpleasant person, and one that we believe turns out deviant behaviour at an impressive rate.[1]

More rewards

There are occasions when praise and other social rewards are not adequate to change a child's behaviour. There are some unhappy children who do not find their parents' positive attention at all rewarding, who seem to get pleasure instead from making those around them angry and upset. These children need different techniques. Again, the sort of behaviour that costs the child a lot of effort may need stronger rewards than praise to keep it going. Tidying up toys and clothes might fall into this category, or giving up a long-established habit, like thumb-sucking or night waking.

For high-cost behaviours like these what works best, for any child from two to three years upwards, is a prominently displayed star-chart system tied in to a pre-arranged treat. The child gets to colour in a square, or stick on a sticker, or draw a smiley face, or uncover a small picture of one of his favourite story/cartoon characters, for each period he manages not to suck his thumb, not to wake you in the night or not to leave any toys on the floor at bedtime. Each time he completes a square of his chart he is also praised. When he reaches a specified number of stars or squares (something you have agreed with him beforehand) you will fulfil your part of the bargain with whatever treat you have jointly decided upon. The chart will look something like this:

The squares can represent days (M, T, W, T, F), or shorter periods (Mon a.m., Mon p.m., Tue a.m.,) or discrete events (for example, a square for each mealtime, or for each visit to granny).

The *form* of the chart, from sticking on a gold star to unveiling Snow White and the Seven Dwarfs one by one, must be carefully chosen to match the child's age and interests. Completing each square is itself intended to be mildly reinforcing, a small token to keep the child going until he earns the big reward.

The length of the chart is the most difficult decision; if it takes too long to earn the reward, the child may well lose interest. A young child's chart should last no more than a few days; a new one can then be drawn up. An older child, working towards a really substantial goal like a new bike, could be expected to operate over a much longer period – for example, a whole term without a note being sent home from the school to the parents about his misbehaviour.

Another decision concerns whether the child must fill up every *consecutive space* on the chart to earn his reward (for example, go a complete week without hitting his sister), or whether he can earn it if he is only partially successful (hit her no more than once in the week). It is best to begin with a target the child can fairly easily meet, and to increase the difficulty over successive charts.

The final reward can be an activity, a trip or a tangible treat. Rewards can include:

- Reading the child a story.
- A trip to the park.
- Going fishing or to a football match with father.
- Staying up late to watch a particular TV programme.
- Having a friend to stay overnight.
- Being allowed to stay out later than usual for a special party.
- One dip into a bag of small, wrapped surprises.
- Buying him an ice cream.
- A game of monopoly.
- Having a favourite meal cooked specially.
- Going swimming, skating, to karate classes.
- A box of chocolates all to himself.

It can be very effective for parent and child together to take a large sheet of paper, divide it into squares and draw in each square a stick figure engaged in an activity the child particularly enjoys and would like to do more often.[2] Pinned up next to the star chart, this serves as a 'menu' from which the child will choose one square when he has completed his chart. If he has any difficulty thinking up ideas for the menu, helpful questions include *people* he would like to spend more time with, *places* where he would like to spend more time, *things* he would like to own and favourite foods and drinks.

Many parents, when first using star-chart systems, are afraid they will have to use them for ever. In practice this rarely turns out to be a problem. Once the chart has focused the family's attention on a new, positive behaviour that behaviour goes on long after the chart has been taken down – either because the parents are still noticing it and praising it occasionally, or because the child has learned new skills (such as alternative non-violent ways to handle quarrels), or because his newly acquired behaviour has its own naturally occurring rewards (such as finding he now has friends). If the behaviour does begin to slip the parents can step in with another star-chart: such top-ups will most probably be needed at some point, but they will often be less elaborate and of shorter duration than the first intervention.

Pitfalls

It is important, when using a reward system, to make it clear to the child that he will never under any circumstances receive a reward if he has previously *asked* to be rewarded, and to apply this rule consistently. Without the rule, it is easy to reach a point where the child says 'If I do X will you give me Y?' or where you are reinforcing a grasping 'I want' attitude. A reward system should be presented to a child as a new way of helping him to learn to do something which you know is hard for him; not as 'If you . . . then I' but rather as 'When you . . . then I'. He should know, too, that it is entirely under your control and not his. You will consult him about the reward and the terms for earning it; ideally this can eventually become a joint exercise in planning, with the child himself setting the next target to aim at. But to begin with, the parent should call the tune. If you have defined the behaviour precisely enough, in readily observable terms, there should be no room for the sort of arguments about whether or not he has earned the reward, and in which he might attempt to bully and cajole. If you are reliable and prompt about giving the reward you will avoid giving him the opportunity to remind you, an opportunity which again might make him feel that he (and not you) was in charge.

What if your reward system does not work? It is important to remember that a positive reward system is not a prescription for a problem, but an *experiment* in changing behaviour. If the experiment is unsuccessful, the parent will look again at the economics of the situation and devise a second experiment. He may hypothesize that praise alone is not a sufficient reinforcer to balance, for example, the effort of completing homework and may institute a points system or a star chart. He should expect, as with many tasks, to need two or three attempts before getting it right. In particular, if a system fails he should check that:

● Reinforcement was clear, contingent and continuous (the three Cs).
● Reinforcement was not too difficult to attain.
● The strength of the reinforcer matched the difficulty the child would experience in changing the behaviour.

Examples: table manners

Louise's parents felt she had very bad table manners, and they spent time at every meal telling her they couldn't bear to watch her, she was revolting, would have to eat in the kitchen by herself. They were encouraged to find out exactly what it was about her eating that bothered them. It emerged that she ate very fast, with her mouth open, and leaned back from the table so that food often spilled. Her parents set her the following targets: to take more than five minutes over each course (timed on a kitchen timer), to close her mouth when chewing and swallowing, and to have spilled nothing on her clothes by the end of each meal. For every mealtime that she fulfilled these conditions, she was praised and drew a small knife and fork in one of three spaces on a chart. Three filled spaces were exchanged for a game of Cluedo in the evening. After three successive charts were completed, the next chart was drawn up – with five spaces, each representing a whole day's meals. Five spaces filled meant a trip to the ice-cream shop at the weekend. No further charts were needed, though Louise's parents continued to praise her for her table manners. Louise's best friend, Catherine, had an opposite problem, she ate too slowly and could take well over half an hour to finish what was on her plate. Catherine's chart, introduced at the same time, involved her taking less than ten minutes to finish a course. The girls enjoyed timing each other on visits to each other's houses, and soon found themselves finishing meals at about the same time.

Tidying up

David and John were, when small, encouraged to help their parents tidy the play room at the end of the day. If either of them did help, they were praised and given a sweet. By the time they were four, both were reliably helping with only an occasional sweet, and by five they were able to do the whole job themselves with a sweet only on the days friends had come to play, when there was more mess than usual. As they grew older and were expected to help with other household chores (make their own beds, help with the washing up), the things they would do were discussed and listed on a chart to be ticked off as completed. An extra few pence of pocket money were given for a completed list, with the possibility of earning more for special 'bonus' tasks like mowing the lawn or washing the car.

Homework

Ben had homework every day but put off doing it. His parents were advised to make a rule that he could not ride his bike, play outside or watch TV until his homework was completed, but they proved unable to enforce the rule. As an alternative, Ben was put on a points system whereby he earned ten points for completing all his assignments; points were exchangeable for 'late' time – an hour of staying up later than usual, which could be used on the day it was earned or saved up for the weekend.[3]

School problems

Mark was constantly in trouble for his behaviour on the school bus. After a meeting between the parents and the school, the following plan was put into action. The bus driver was supplied with pretyped notes stating that Mark had not been out of his seat or got into fights on the bus. If Mark met these conditions, he was to be given a note. The note was redeemable at home for a daily activity of Mark's choice, with his father. After two weeks of perfect behaviour, reinforcement was thinned to a weekend activity with the father if Mark obtained four out of five good behaviour notes in a week, and finally to a weekend activity in return for a gold note from the driver indicating that he had behaved well all week on the bus.[1]

Nichola's teacher complained to her parents that she was not doing any work in class. He agreed to make a daily note in her homework book of the amount of effort she had put into her work that day on a points scale ranging from zero to five. Her parents noted the points over a two-week period and worked out that her daily average was between zero and one point. They agreed with her that, if she could raise that daily average to at least one point over the next week, she could have a friend to stay the night at the weekend. This achieved, the goal was raised to two points. Nichola's teacher was pleased with her improvement and began to be able to find opportunities to praise her work; the relationship between them improved. Nichola herself suggested that she would like to aim at a four-point average; she failed the first week but succeeded the next, being reinforced with enrolment in a Saturday dance class she had been asking about for some time.

Toilet training

Joanna, aged four, had been potty trained at two but relapsed and began to wet her pants at least once a day, usually when too busy to bother to go to the toilet. After weeks of mild scoldings and even the odd smack, her mother began to check her pants regularly during the day and give her a Smartie whenever the pants were dry. The wetting soon stopped, and it was possible to move on to checking and rewarding only once, at bedtime.

Michelle, aged three, soiled herself. She hated to use the toilet or potty and would hold on to her motions for days, with eventual severe constipation and unpleasant leakage into her pants. Her problem was making it difficult for her to settle in playgroup. Her mother was advised to keep her at home for a few days and give her lots of fruit and fibrous cereals, potting her regularly during the day and rewarding successes with a small eggcupful of sweets; these were a great treat as she was seldom allowed them. To her mother's surprise Michelle's problem cleared up straight away.

Overactivity

Peter was an energetic four-year-old, happiest in active, fast-moving play, especially outdoors. He had never shown any interest in listening to stories, doing puzzles, playing with Lego or any other game that needed settled concentration. He was shortly to start school and his parents were worried about how he would cope. His mother set aside a period each day when she would take him on her lap and tell or read him a story; she began with a very short story to go with a photo from the family album and worked up slowly to picture books, then traditional repetitive folk tales. Peter's father set aside a period when Peter and he played side by side with constructional toys, at first for only a few minutes but later for longer. Peter was praised whenever possible for 'sitting quietly'. He spent a short time each day with jigsaw puzzles and his mother would set a kitchen timer on these occasions, explaining that if he could sit quietly and work on the puzzle until the timer rang he could have a piece of cheese, which he loved. Peter enjoyed this game and it was possible to extend the timer interval by stages from five to fifteen minutes.

Contracts

Contracts[5,6] are formalized, written reward systems; they detail the privileges which an individual will gain after fulfilling clearly defined responsibilities. They are most useful with teenagers. This is an example of a typical contract.[7]

Sharon Smith

1 In exchange for going into town after school – Sharon will be home by 5.30.
2 In exchange for going out between 11.30 a.m. and 5.30 p.m. at weekends – Sharon will tidy her room and help with the breakfast dishes before leaving.
3 In exchange for telephoning her boyfriend daily – Sharon will complete her homework.
4 In exchange for going out one weekend evening till 11.00 p.m. – Sharon will let her parents know where she is going and will bring home no bad behaviour notes from school in the previous week.

If Sharon complies with all four conditions in any week, she will be entitled to a bonus privilege, chosen from the following:

● Permission to go out on one other weekend evening.
● An extra £1 credited to her clothing allowance.
● One credit towards the twenty needed for her to be allowed to give a party at home for her friends.

All contracts should have a bonus clause; some also incorporate fixed penalties for failure to comply, as in this example:

Danny

	M	T	W	T	F
Gets to school on time (2 points)					
Arrives home by 5 p.m. (2 points)					
Does not fight with his sister (5 points)					
Does not swear (2 points)					
Puts dirty clothes in laundry basket (2 points)					
Does his homework (5 points)					

> If Danny gets 16 points or more in any one day he will not have to help wash up after dinner and can choose the TV programmes that evening.
>
> If Danny gets less than 13 points he will have to help with the dinner dishes.
>
> If Danny gets less than 10 points he will have to do the dishes by himself.
>
> If Danny gets less than 7 points he will have to do the dishes and will not be allowed to watch TV that evening.

Contracts are intended to reduce friction between the adolescent and his parents. They require joint negotiation but, once this has been achieved, they make the rules and penalties sufficiently clear to all parties so that there is no room for further argument. They are well worth trying when the normal channels of communication seem to have broken down and the parents find themselves pushed into an increasingly hostile and punitive stance.

References

1 G. R. Patterson, S. McNeal, N. Hawkins and R. Phelps, 'Reprogramming the social environment', *J. Child Psychol. Psychiatry*, 8 (1967), 181–95.
2 R. M. Addison and L. E. Homme, 'The reinforcing event (RE) menu', *National Society for Programmed Instruction Journal*, 5 (1966), 8–9.
3 G. J. Blackham and A. Silberman, *Modification of Child Behaviour*, California, Wadsworth Publishing, 1971.
4 R. G. Tharp and R. J. Wetzel, *Behaviour Modification in the Natural Environment*, New York and London, Academic Press, 1969.
5 J. F. Alexander and B. V. Parsons, 'Short-term behavioural intervention and delinquent families', *J. Abnorm. Psychol.*, 81 (1973), 219–25.
6 L. Weathers and R. P. Liberman, 'Contingency contracting with families of delinquent adolescents', *Behav. Therapy*, 6 (1975), 356–66.
7 R. B. Stuart, 'Behavioural contracting with the families of delinquents', *J. Behav. Therapy and Exptal. Psychiatry*, 2 (1971), 1–11.
8 G. R. Patterson, *Families: Applications of Social Learning to Family Life*, Champaign, Illinois, Research Press, 1971.

6 Punishment

Most parents smack their children sometimes – ninety-seven per cent in the Newsons' Nottingham Study.[1] Half of these mothers said they only smacked in anger, but half used smacking more deliberately as a disciplinary technique. Yet despite the widespread use of physical punishment, many parents feel a sense of guilt when they smack, and many wonder whether punishment – in the sense of applying psychologically or physically painful consequences to a child's misbehaviour – is really a good idea.

The purpose of this chapter is not to debate the morality or ethics of punishment. It will, however, present the evidence from psychological research on whether punishment is effective and whether it has any side effects. It will also look at the other ways in which parents commonly respond when a child misbehaves.

Physical punishment

Laboratory studies of the effects of painful stimuli have mainly, for obvious reasons, been done with animal subjects. Interpreting such research needs to be done with caution, since the similarities between electric shock applied to rats and a quick smack applied to a two-year-old are very small. Most physical punishment used by parents is not intended to be, or experienced as, particularly painful; it is, rather, a symbol and signal of displeasure. It is, as the Newsons put it, part of a system of communication between parent and child; it usually comes at the end of a chain of behavioural events and carries a simple parental message: 'I have had enough.'

In this context there is no evidence that the odd smack does any harm and some evidence that occasional resort to power – assertive techniques like smacking, against a background of otherwise warm 'inductive' (reasoning-oriented) techniques, can be effective.[2] Most parents do switch between the two styles of discipline with no apparent ill-effects.[3]

There is general agreement, from both laboratory and field studies, that punishment does 'work' in the sense that it will suppress most behaviours quickly and – *if* an alternative positive behaviour is available and is rewarded – completely.[4] It does, however, have certain drawbacks.

First, it may suppress the behaviour only in the presence of the person who has done the punishing. It does *not* contribute to the development of internalized moral standards or conscience. If the parent smacks Jane for taking sweets from the supermarket check-out, she may take care not to do it again when the parent is there but, if the parent is not there, she may succumb to temptation.

Second, it does not teach the child what she should do instead of the undesirable act. In some emergency situations, as when the child is touching an electric plug or running out into the street in traffic, this may not matter very much. The parents' aim is simply to stop the child from engaging in potentially dangerous behaviour, not to teach alternatives. But in other instances, such as quarrelling over toys, the parent wants her to learn how to share and take turns: smacking here will not help, and may indeed hinder because it produces a state of high emotional arousal that interferes with new learning.[5]

Third, punishment in any form, and physical punishment in particular, may have side effects. It may lead the child to dislike and avoid the agent of punishment, to 'turn off' or 'tune out' from the teacher or parent who punishes her. It may lead to counter-aggression (mild as in a passive refusal to comply with instructions, or severe as in a physical attack on the agent of punishment); such counter-aggression often provokes more intense punishment and a spiralling interaction ensues.[6] It may provide an aggressive model for the child to imitate; as we saw earlier there is impressive evidence that parents who use a lot of physical punishment tend to have children who are more aggressive than normal.[7,8]

Despite these drawbacks, smacking has been successfully 'prescribed' in the treatment of some problem children, particularly for very defiant children whose parents have been totally unable to control them in the past – like Jeff, whom we met in chapter 1.[9]

> The first stage in Jeff's rehabilitation was to teach his mother to ignore him when he sulked, shouted or hit her. If ignoring such abuse did not stop him, she was to tell him in a very angry manner to stop, and finally, if he persisted, she was to spank him. She had spanked him very severely in the past when she reached the end of her tether, but the spanking had not been associated in any systematic way with things Jeff had or had not done. The mother was also shown how to praise Jeff very warmly for all

his acceptable behaviour, and to tell him why he was praised. She was able after some practice to carry out these instructions; for example, in one observation session she first asked Jeff to sit down next to her and, when he refused, she told him again with anger to sit down, ignoring it when he swore at her and bit her hand, and finally smacking him. It was during this session that Jeff asked 'Are you angry?', just after a third spanking.

Several weeks later Jeff was behaving very much better. His mother reported that she now hardly needed to smack him, since her angry voice had come to carry a warning. As an example of his improvement, she quoted an exchange where Jeff told her to stop singing along with the radio in the car. She realized that she was being controlled by him and told him firmly that she would sing any time she wanted to. Jeff begged her to stop and even asked 'Why can't you stop when I tell you?' She went on singing. Later, when she was choosing doughnuts from a drive-in restaurant, Jeff questioned her choice only once, ending with 'OK, mother, whatever you feel like.' The mother reported that she was beginning to like Jeff much more, and that he was expressing affection for her for almost the first time in his life.

Verbal punishment

Although it is probably the most widely used form of discipline, there has been little research concentrating exclusively on the effects of shouting at children. There is some work[10,11] which shows that parents of aggressive boys use more nagging, scolding and ridicule than other parents, and in chapter 4 we saw that verbal reprimands were much less effective in a variety of settings than other techniques. Again, however, there are degrees of verbal punishment as there are of physical punishment and, while the complex of nagging/mild scolding/threats may be ineffective, we need more evidence on the effects of really loud, convincing verbal punishment – the kind of 'no' which parents can produce when they see their child about to poke her fingers in an electric socket. Very angry reprimands may well function similarly to smacking in suppressing a behaviour quickly and efficiently; like Jeff's mother, some parents may find showing anger in the voice a useful skill to practise.

How to punish if you have to

Punishment should be immediate to be effective; it has, moreover, the strongest suppressive effects if an act is punished just as it gets under way, rather than after it is over – tapping the child's finger just as she moves to pull the cat's tail, rather than just after she has pulled it. This was demonstrated in an intriguing set of experiments by Dr Justin Aronfreed at Pennsylvania University.[12] In these experiments, with nine- and ten-year-old children, a pair of toys was shown to the child – one a particularly attractive and interesting toy, of the kind most children would want to touch (such as a tiny electric motor, or a camera with moving parts) and one with much less appeal (a thimble, a hair slide). The experimenter asked the child to pick up and talk about one toy, using a mild punishment if she chose the more attractive of the pair. The nature and timing of the punishment would vary: in some experiments the child was allowed to pick up the camera and then a loud buzzer would sound; in others the experimenter might take away some sweets the child had previously been given; in others he might say 'no' just as the child was reaching for the attractive toy. After ten or so such trials, the experimenter made an excuse to leave the room, after putting out a pair of toys. The child was observed through a screen to see if she would pick up the more attractive 'forbidden' toy; in other words whether she would resist temptation. The extent of resistance to temptation was taken as a measure of the effectiveness of the punishment condition used.

Children who had been punished just as they reached for the attractive toy showed greater resistance to temptation than children punished just after they had picked it up, or several seconds later. The effects of punishment several *hours* later (as in the 'wait till your father comes home' approach) were not, however, examined, and it is possible that this can work with older children, as long as they are reminded at the time of punishment of what they did wrong. For young children, to 'catch them in the act' should be the aim.

Another of Aronfreed's experiments showed how important it is if punishment is to be at all effective, for the child to understand clearly what she is doing wrong and what she can do instead. In this experiment one group of children learned to choose the less attractive of two toys in pairs where the forbidden toy was always of one colour, and easy to identify. A second group was shown pairs where there were no colour cues. When an unpleasant sharp sound was used as the punishment, the second group, who had the more difficult discrimination to make, learned much less effectively; they became anxious and disorganized. Some children, frequently slapped and shouted at for no very clear reason, are placed in a similar real-life dilemma by their parents. *Clear* rules, often repeated and consistently applied, are the necessary starting point for any kind of punishment.

Again, it is worth bearing in mind the finding that punishment works best against a background of warmth between parent and child.[13] If you and the child have a good relationship, it will survive the odd smack but, if you are not getting on well, then you should look at other ways of handling misbehaviour. *Frequent* punishment has more side effects than infrequent, so that you should also reconsider your methods if you find yourself smacking and shouting very often.

Finally, what you do after you have punished the child is as important as the punishment itself. Many parents feel so guilty and uncomfortable after losing their temper that they feel obliged to make up for it to the child, with anything from long attention-giving chats to extra cuddles or a packet of sweets. Children soon catch on to this; the eventual reward cancels out any effects of punishment and misbehaviour is likely to increase rather than decrease.

Withdrawal of privileges

Withdrawing privileges or material rewards is another common parental reaction, used or threatened by sixty-nine per cent of the Newsons' Nottingham parents:[1] 'You've been naughty, now I won't let you play outside . . . go to the football match . . . have that biscuit.' Laboratory studies show that withdrawal of rewards can be effective in suppressing behaviour. In one experiment,[14] for example, children were rewarded with candy for co-operative responses in a lever-pressing task; later one member of each pair ceased to be rewarded for co-operating, or both children lost candies for the co-operative response. Taking candy away had a more rapid and long-term effect on the level of co-operation than did simple non-reward. In another study,[15] children were shown a film; as they watched they could press a bar to obtain some peanuts. When they had learned to do this, the conditions were changed so that either bar-pressing produced no peanuts or the film stopped every time they pressed the bar. Again, withdrawing reward (interrupting the film) was highly effective.

Parents can use similar methods in the home; for example, as part of a programme to stop a child sucking her thumb (see chapter 12) they can switch off the television briefly every time they see the child sucking while she is watching TV, or if she is misbehaving at a mealtime they can take her plate away for a few minutes.

Field studies on withdrawal of privileges and reward are, however, less encouraging than those in the laboratory. It has been found, for example, that parents of aggressive boys make more use of these techniques than do other parents:[10] frequent use of deprivation was associated with high use of physical punishment and with cold, rejecting attitudes. Another study showed that mothers of 'likeable' children rarely used deprivation of privileges.[16] It is possible that again we are seeing effects rather than causes: difficult, aggressive children calling for stronger control techniques from their parents than do easy children. It seems likely, however, that frequently taking things away from the child or thwarting her expectations could produce high levels of frustration, counter-aggression and hostility towards the parent. It is probably a technique best used sparingly.

It can be made more acceptable to the child, and more effective, if the parent gives first before he or she takes away. If, for example, you want to stop your child swearing, you can give her an *extra* twenty pence on her

Saturday pocket money and tell her that every time she swears she must put five pence from this special fund into the family swearing box.[6]

As with all disciplinary techniques, it is important to follow through on any threats or promises. Very often parents threaten to withdraw a reward or privilege of such magnitude and importance to the child (going to a birthday party or a pantomime, for example) that, when it comes to it, they feel unable to face the child's disappointment and fall into the 'oh all right then, but *next* time you . . .' trap. Threatening to cancel major treats is best avoided altogether.

Reasoning with the child

Laboratory and field studies on the effects of reasoning with children agree that this is on the whole a 'good thing', and that in particular it promotes the development of conscience. Aronfreed demonstrated that children given a *reason* for choosing the less attractive of the two toys (told, for example, that the other toy was really meant for older children as they would be more able to describe it) showed much greater resistance to temptation than children who were punished in the same way but not told why. Very many researchers have found that children who operate from internalized standards and who feel guilty when they transgress prohibitions have had most exposure to disciplinary techniques that point out the effects of their behaviour on others.[17] Their parents, on seeing the child try to carry off a teddy bear from a friend's house, will react strongly: 'If you take that, Jane will be so sad when she can't hug him at bedtime.' They discuss aggression: 'If you push her, she will fall down and hurt herself.' They stress reparation: 'You've broken Simon's car; you must give him one of yours in exchange', 'You've hurt Rachel; now tell her you're very sorry'. If they issue a prohibition, they explain the reason: 'You can't play outside because it will be dark very soon'.

The use of reasoning techniques like these does not necessarily have an effect on the child's *immediate* compliance. In the long term, however, they do foster obedience;[18] they are associated with low levels of aggression in children;[10] they increase the probability that the child will do the right thing in the absence of adult surveillance.[19]

The only possible pitfall with reasoning is one of timing. Long discussions with children about right and wrong, consequences and reparation, involve large amounts of parental attention. They can inadvertently reward the child for the very misbehaviour the parent wishes to stop. This issue will be further discussed in chapter 14, in the context of handling arguments between brothers and sisters; for the moment we should note that there may be occasions when it is best to postpone discussion of moral issues until well *after* the event.

References

1 J. Newson and E. Newson, *Four Years Old in an Urban Community*, London, Allen and Unwin, 1968.
2 M. L. Hoffman, 'Moral internalization: current theory and research', in L. Berkowitz (ed.), *Advances in Experimental Social Psychology*, vol. 10, New York, Academic Press, 1977.
3 J. E. Grusec and L. Kuczynski, 'Direction of effect in socialization: a comparison of parents' versus the child's behaviour as determinants of disciplinary techniques', *Dev. Psychol.*, 16 (1980), 1–9.
4 N. H. Azrin and W. C. Holz, 'Punishment', in W. K. Honig (ed.), *Operant behaviour: Areas of Research and Application*, New York, Appleton-Century-Crofts, 1966.
5 B. F. Skinner, *Science and Human Behaviour*, New York, MacMillan, 1953.
6 R. G. Tharp and R. J. Wetzel, *Behaviour Modification in the Natural Environment*, New York and London, Academic Press, 1969.
7 W. C. Becker, 'Consequences of different kinds of parental discipline', in M. L. Hoffman and L. W. Hoffman (eds), *Review of Child Development Research*, vol. I, New York, Russell Sage Foundation, 1964.
8 S. Feshbach, 'Aggression', in P. H. Mussen (ed.), *Carmichael's Manual of Child Psychology*, 3rd edn., vol. 2, London, Wiley, 1970.
9 M. E. Bernal, J. S. Duryee, H. L. Pruett and B. J. Burns, 'Behaviour modification and the brat syndrome', *J. Consult. Clin. Psychol*, 32 (1968), 447–55.
10 A. Bandura and R. H. Walters, *Adolescent Aggression*, New York, Ronald, 1959.
11 G. R. Patterson, *Coercive Family Process*, Eugene, Oregon, Castalia, 1982.
12 J. Aronfreed and A. Reber, 'Internalized behavioural suppression and the timing of social punishment', *J. Personality and Social Psychol.*, 1 (1965), 3–16.
13 R. R. Sears, E. E. Maccoby and H. Levin, *Patterns of Child Rearing*, Evanston, Illinois, Row Peterson, 1957.
14 H. P. Weingold and R. L. Webster, 'Effects of punishment on a co-operative behaviour in children', *Child Dev.*, 35 (1964), 1211–16.
15 D. M. Baer, 'A technique of social reinforcement for the study of child behaviour', *Child Dev.*, 33 (1962), 847–58.
16 C. L. Winder and L. Rau, 'Parental attitudes associated with social deviance in pre-adolescent boys', *J. Abnormal and Social Psychol.*, 64 (1962), 418–24.
17 M. L. Hoffman, 'Moral development', in P. H. Mussen (ed.), *Manual of Child Psychology*, 3rd edn., vol. 2, London, Wiley, 1970.
18 C. Minton, J. Kagan and J. A. Levine, 'Maternal control and obedience in the two-year-old child', *Child Dev.*, 42 (1971), 1873–94.
19 E. E. Maccoby and J. A. Martin, 'Socialization in the context of the family: parent–child interaction', in E. M. Hetherington (ed.), *Socialization, Personality and Social Development*, vol. IV, *Handbook of Child Psychology*, 4th edn., New York, Wiley, 1983.

7 Alternatives to punishment

If reasoning helps in the long term but does not immediately stop a child from misbehaving, and punishment has undesirable side effects, the next question is whether psychological theory has anything better to offer in the way of handling children's problem behaviour. In this chapter we will look at several alternative research-based approaches which do increasingly look like useful additions to the everyday parent's repertoire.

Ignoring misbehaviour

In an earlier chapter we saw how teachers could reduce the amount of misbehaviour in their classroom simply by not paying any attention to it, responding only to children who were attending to their work. Countless studies have demonstrated that parents can use a similar technique to equally good effect.

Anyone who has ever watched the rapidly escalating mischief of a two- or three-year-old who perceives that his mother is busy talking to her friend and not to him will be aware that children do sometimes misbehave in order to gain attention. Anyone who has experienced their child's irritating habits (from grinding teeth to leaving crusts) will be aware of the truth of the maxim 'he only does it to annoy, because he knows it teases'.

For behaviours like these, whose purpose is to provoke attention, punishment in any form is often less effective than ignoring. The standard advice to parents on how to react – or rather not react – when the child tries out swear words at home is based on this principle. Tantrums, whining and badgering ('can I . . . can I . . . oh why can't I? . . . oh, please') can also all be handled in this way:

John, aged four, annoyed his parents (his father in particular) by bursting into tears after every mild frustration; he was teased by his peers who called him a crybaby. It was suggested to his mother that she note down for a few days what she did when he cried. Her diary showed that she tended to stop what she was doing immediately and make quite a fuss of him. He was accustomed, for example, to having an elastoplast on every little hurt. The diary helped the mother to change her behaviour; she decided to check quickly whether there was any serious cause for concern and, if not, to ignore his crying while paying more attention to him at other times. Crying episodes decreased from an average of eight an hour in the first few days to less than one a day one week later.

A small boy, aged twenty-one months, was in the habit of having a tantrum unless his parents remained in his room until he had gone to sleep. He had been quite ill a few months earlier, and this was when the parents had begun to stay with him. Now he would not let them stop. The parents asked for help and were strongly advised to put the child to bed in a relaxed, unhurried way and then leave, not returning if he cried. It took ten evenings, but by the tenth he went to sleep without tears. Unfortunately a few days later when his aunt was putting him to bed he did cry again briefly, and she agreed to stay in the room with him. The next night he cried loud and long again, and it took his parents a further nine sessions before he gave up his crying. After that, however, there were no further problems.[1]

Paul, aged four and a half, had regular tantrums at his nursery school. The teachers usually held him closely and spoke calmly to him during a tantrum; most tantrums lasted about five minutes. One week however, the teacher's aide took the other children out into the playground when Paul first showed signs of tantrumming; his teacher stationed herself just outside the door and kept an eye on him in silence. When he quietened, she put her head round the door and asked if he was ready to go out into the playground with the others. But this started him off again and she withdrew until he was again quiet. This took twenty-five minutes. The next day he had another fifteen-minute tantrum, but after that there were no more.

These examples make clear that ignoring a child's behaviour is by no means an easy way out; it takes a good deal of determination. A single parent might find it impossible to ignore night crying or daytime tantrums without enlisting help; two people can support each other and take turns for example to leave the house for a while when the child is testing out his power against theirs.

Ignoring crying, whining and tantrums is particularly difficult because at first the child will intensify his efforts to gain attention he is used to. Paul's tantrums increased from five to twenty-five and fifteen minutes before he gave up; John's initial response when his mother ignored him was to cry more loudly and more often. It is essential to be prepared for this initial increase in the very behaviour you want to get rid of, when you begin to ignore it.

It is also essential to be sure before you begin that you will ignore the behaviour *every* time it occurs and continue to ignore it until it stops. If you go in and pick up your crying toddler after he has cried for half an hour, you have made your situation worse, since you have taught him that crying for a long time will pay off in the end. If you ignore the child when he whines for sweets at the supermarket checkout but give in when he begins a full-scale tantrum, you have taught him that, if whining does not work, a proper tantrum will. If you ignore him nine times out of ten that he has a tantrum for sweets but give in just one time, you will have given him the once-in-a-while reward which we saw in chapter 4 will establish a habit more effectively than a reward given every time. He is more likely to cry for sweets in the future if given them one time in ten than if given them every time. Similarly, on the once-in-a-while principle, *one* lapse in a policy of not allowing the child to come into your bed at night will ensure weeks more of night waking. These things cannot always be helped; the child is ill perhaps and you take him into your bed to comfort him, or you are tired and cannot face a battle over sweets that day. But it can be useful to understand why lapses like these have such long-lasting effects, and to avoid them if you possibly can.

Lastly, it is important to avoid any overall reduction in the amount of attention given to the child. Returning him politely to his own room in the small hours needs to be balanced by making a fuss of him in the morning anytime he hasn't disturbed you in the night; ignoring moans means praising him for being cheerful and good company. Withholding the reward of attention for undesirable behaviour must be only one part of a dual strategy, in which the other is a positive reward system for good behaviour.

Time out

There are many situations where ignoring misbehaviour is impractical, dangerous or simply unsuccessful: situations where the child is likely to hurt himself, or others, or where the rewards he gets for his behaviour have nothing to do with your attention. Straightforward disobedience, the 'no I won't' response, is also often not amenable to the ignoring strategy.[2] In these situations, psychologists working with problem children have found a technique called 'time out' (an abbreviation of 'time out from rein-forcement') to be a very successful alternative.

Time out in the home setting means an immediate, calm, no-comment removal of the child from the scene of the crime, and a fixed period of a few minutes which he spends alone in the least interesting spot in the house (often the bathroom, unless he is very young and loves to play with water). Time out is not intended to be a punishment; the idea is to make sure that the child misses out on whatever satisfactions and rewards he would normally obtain from his misbehaviour. For example, if he has hit a playmate there could be several such satisfactions: seeing the other child cry, bringing mother running from the kitchen to sort out the quarrel, getting his way in whatever argument sparked the aggression. If his mother swiftly and soundlessly removes him to the downstairs cloakroom and leaves him there for a few minutes (holding the door handle if necessary), he is denied any reward. Eventually, after repeated occasions in which time out is systematically and consistently applied, he will stop hitting.

Like positive reward systems, time out is practical, and it works. Pitfalls to avoid are:

- Using a room that offers interesting things to do. Time out must be bland, and boring. If you are using a bathroom, clear away bottles and jars first. If a spare bedroom, take away books and ornaments. Don't use the child's own bedroom if at all possible.

- Using too long a time-out period, or a period which varies with your mood. The idea is not to keep the child out of the way until you can stand to see him again. A short, fixed period helps make the situation familiar, predictable and acceptable to the child. Research suggests that over and above about two or three minutes, lengthening the time-out period does not increase its effectiveness. Many parents find three minutes for a pre-school child and five minutes for older children are enough.

- Accompanying time out with punitive comments and lectures. These can be rewarding – the aim is to take the child to time out, or to tell him to go, as unemotionally as you can manage. Reasoning with him about the rights and wrongs of his behaviour should be postponed until later in the day. Avoid making any sort of fuss of him after the time out; simply open the door, or call 'time's up' and leave it at that.

- Using time out long after the event. If the child misbehaves while you are out, it will not help to say 'It's the bathroom for you when we get home.' Try to find some other way of isolating him temporarily – on a chair with his back to playmates, or outside the room, or in your car.

A good example of the use of time out is the case of Peter:[3]

> Peter was four years old, very disobedient and always having tantrums. If frustrated he would kick, hit, pull off or tear his clothes and shout abuse. His mother found him completely unmanageable. Her usual method of coping with his misbehaviour was reasoning with him or trying to distract him. She did sometimes put him in his high chair for short periods but continued to argue and reason with him throughout the tantrum which

inevitably followed. Peter was observed at home and nine categories of misbehaviour (for example throwing objects, pushing his sister) were identified; his mother was instructed to tell Peter firmly to stop if he did any of these things. If he persisted she was to place him in his bedroom (from which all toys and playthings had been removed) for five minutes. Additionally, she was to praise and cuddle him for specified positive behaviours. Peter tested his mother, and the treatment team, to the limit in the first few sessions; he broke a window in his bedroom during time out and called out that he had cut himself. His mother checked that the cut was very minor, swept up the glass, then left. After six hour-long sessions in which time out was used every time he misbehaved, Peter's objectionable behaviours dropped to a stable level of two to eight per session, compared with the twenty to a hundred he had shown before intervention. The improvement was maintained over a follow-up period; the mother reported that she was now using time out approximately once a week, felt more sure of herself, and more affectionate towards her son.

Logical consequences

Another variant of psychological learning theory, using natural and logical consequences to deal with misbehaviour, is a technique invented by Rudolf Dreikurs and his associates in America. It is described in his invaluable book for parents called *Children: The Challenge*[4] and in a similar volume for teachers.[5] The basic principle of the technique is that much of a child's misbehaviour has consequences he might not like, and that, *if* we can allow him to experience these consequences (short of any which might cause him real harm), he will learn from the situation without lectures, scoldings or punishment. Here are some examples of these natural consequences:

- The child doesn't eat his lunch: he feels hungry all afternoon.
- The child won't get up when his alarm goes in the morning: he misses the school bus, is late for school and is told off by his teacher.
- The child forgets to listen to what the homework is: it doesn't get done and he has to explain why at school next day.
- The child loses a favourite toy: it doesn't get replaced, unless he chooses to use his own pocket money to buy a new one.
- The child won't put dirty clothes in the laundry basket: they don't get washed, and the day comes when the favourite dress isn't there for the girl to wear, or the boy has to go to school in two different-coloured socks.

If you look at what you do in situations like these, you will probably find you usually protect your child in some way from natural consequences. You let him have a snack mid-afternoon if he didn't eat lunch. You wake him in the morning and hurry him into his clothes so he will catch the school bus. You telephone a friend to ask what the homework should be when your child forgets. You hate to see him so sad when he has lost a toy he really cares for and, though you deliver a lecture about taking care of possessions, you still end up getting him a new one. You pick up his clothes for him when he's nearly out of clean socks. You feel somehow that, if you didn't do these things, you would be letting him down. What you are really doing, very often, is protecting yourself from the pain of seeing your child unhappy or socially embarrassed. You will be helping him more if you don't protect yourself and him, but simply allow logical consequences to take their course.

Sometimes there are no obvious natural consequences for the child's behaviour. With a little thought you may find you can arrange some. If you are in the habit of reading to your child at bedtime, you could point out that you won't have time tonight because you have to spend the reading time tidying up the toys he hasn't put away. If your children quarrel incessantly in the car, you might let them know this means you can't concentrate on your driving and will have to pull off the road and sit for a while until they have finished their argument (this is more likely to work on the way to the beach than to the dentist, of course). If your child does not come when called for dinner, he may find his food has been thrown away or given to the dog: if he does not come, after all, it makes sense to assume he is not hungry. If he is particularly grouchy all afternoon, you assume he is tired and needs to go to bed early to catch up on sleep.

Logical consequences should never be used as a threat or imposed in anger. The parent doesn't need to say 'If you don't eat your lunch, you'll be hungry later' – the child will find this out himself. Nor do you need to say, when he asks for biscuits mid-afternoon, 'You see, you're hungry now, I told you you would be.' You should simply say 'I'm sorry if you're hungry, but it's not dinner time yet.' Remember that if he is hungry, that is his problem and not yours. He will do his best to make life unpleasant for you until dinner time, but it is important that you withstand whatever emotional blackmail he has learned to use to get his own way.

References

1 C. D. Williams, 'The elimination of tantrum behaviour by extinction procedures', *J. Abnormal and Social Psychology*, 59 (1959), 269.
2 R. G. Wahler, 'Oppositional children: a quest for parental reinforcement control', *J. Applied Behav. Analysis.*, 2 (1969), 159–70.
3 R. Hawkins, R. Peterson, E. Schweid and S. Bijou, 'Behaviour therapy in the home: amelioration of problem parent–child relationships with the parent in the therapeutic role', *J. Exptal. Child Psychol.*, 4 (1966), 99–107.
4 R. Dreikurs, *Children: The Challenge*, New York, Hawthorn-Dutton, 1964.
5 R. Dreikurs, B. Grunwald and F. Pepper, *Maintaining Sanity in the Classroom*, New York, Harper Row, 1971.

8 Communication I

The reader who picked up this book in the hope that it would help him, or her, to understand children's feelings and motives – their 'psychology' in the popular sense of the word – may until now have been disappointed. The previous chapters have concentrated almost exclusively on the child's external behaviour, and not her inner world. They have described some useful, but perhaps mechanical, ways of handling her behaviour or misbehaviour, without reference to *why* she might be behaving in that particular way. For most parents this is rightly not enough; they want to understand why the child acts as she does, and if she is unhappy or anxious or angry they want to help.

One of the propositions in this book is that we do not *always* need to know why children do certain things; that not all their troublesome behaviour necessarily has a deep 'psychological' cause. We have seen, for example, how a child's disturbed sleep, or temper tantrums, may be a simple consequence of learning; the child wakes because it was warm and cosy in her parents' bed last night, and not because she is anxious or troubled. We have seen that she may demand an undue amount of attention, not because her unfortunate parents have deprived or neglected her in some way (as their child-care manual may tell them) but because she has confidently learned to expect such attention in the past – because she was a colicky baby perhaps and simply got used to having adults pick her up and play with her for much of the day.

Nevertheless this kind of analysis is not always enough. There are many occasions when we do need to look to the child's inner world, and many occasions when her troublesome behaviour is a way of asking us to try and understand how she is feeling at a particular time. One of the notions shared by all who work professionally with troubled children is that their symptoms are a kind of communication, a cry for help; parents too can usefully look at some of their children's everyday problem behaviours in a similar light.

In this chapter we will look first at some of these problem behaviours (with the exception of fears, habits and aggression which are separately examined in chapters 11 to 13) to see whether they are likely to be 'a cry for help' from the child; in other words, whether they are normal developmental stages which every child goes through, or whether they should be seen as cause for concern. In the chapter which follows we will consider how a parent can go about understanding what might be troubling a child if she is showing signs of needing help: at the motives and concerns which predominate at different stages in the child's life, at the events which she may experience as stressful, and at effective and ineffective ways of communicating with a child who has something on her mind.

Common childhood problems: sleep disorders

Disturbances of sleep and difficulty in settling to sleep are very common in the preschool years: surveys,[1,2] for example, report that twenty-one per cent of two-and-a-half-year-olds have bedtime or sleep problems, that thirteen per cent of three-year-olds have difficulty in settling and that fourteen per cent wake in the night. While it can happen that stress (such as the birth of a sibling)[3] can contribute to the problem, such difficulties often show a consistent pattern from early infancy and may reflect individual differences in temperament.[4] Sleep disorders in young children *should* be tackled; Jo Douglas and Naomi Richman's sensible and practical book *My Child won't Sleep*[5] shows parents how to go about this. But they are not necessarily symptoms of distress.

Sleep disturbance in older children is less common. By four years only eight per cent of children wake regularly in the night, and by eight years only three per cent of children have any sleep problem;[6] in this sense a spell of disturbed sleep may suggest that something is bothering the child. If she can't settle to sleep (ten per cent of eight-year-olds have this problem) she may simply need firmer limits about going to bed and staying there, or she may need less sleep than she used to, or she may have things on her mind. Only experiment can tell you which.

Nightmares can be a sign of anxiety but are very common, particularly in three- and four-year-olds. They call for comforting but should not worry the parent unduly unless there are signs of upset in the daytime as well. Night terrors, as distinct from nightmares, are very frightening for parents: the child half wakes from deep sleep with a cry; she is pale and her breathing is fast and irregular. Such terrors are not, however, associated with daytime anxiety and are considered psychiatrically normal[7] – though they can increase when the child is mildly stressed as after moving house or changing school. Sleep-walking shows a similar increase at these times but is quite common (some fifteen per cent of five-to-twelve-year-olds regularly walk in their sleep) and shows no general association with emotional disturbance; there is some evidence that it runs in families.[8]

Explanations of sleep disorders in psychodynamic terms suggest that they may spring from the child's inner jealous and angry thoughts. If a child is experiencing many such thoughts and has not been able to express them, the theory goes, her nights may be troubled by dreams of bogeymen who will punish her for what she sees as her badness. The wicked witches and ogres of nightmare are seen as the loving mother and father transmuted by the child's fear of retribution; such figures might occur in the child's dreams at times when she is experiencing most conflict with parents in the daytime. This theory might explain why the immediate preschool years are the peak period for nightmares – the three-to-four-year-old being prone to some very turbulent feelings whilst at the same time just developing a sense of right and wrong. Other theorists see sleep problems as having to do with a fear of the helplessness and vulnerability implied by falling asleep or with confusions (sometimes after a death in the family) between sleep and dying which make the child fear she might not wake up again.

Bedwetting and soiling

Fifty per cent of three-year-olds and thirty per cent of four-year-olds wet the bed regularly; these figures slowly decrease until by nine years old only two per cent of girls and three per cent of boys still wet once a week or more. Wetting up to the age of three is entirely normal, but children who wet after that age differ qualitatively in that more, though by no means all, will show other behaviour problems, and in that, if they wet at four, they may well continue doing so for several years.[9] Bedwetting very often runs in families[10] and may be related to physical abnormalities of the bladder.[11] It *is* associated with a greater risk of psychiatric problems (particularly in girls) and with the experience of stress: one study[12] found that children who had more stressful life events at three to four years were twice as likely to become enuretic as those who experienced less stress. It used to be thought that secondary enuresis (that is, bedwetting beginning after the child has previously been dry) was more likely to reflect stress and anxiety than primary enuresis (where the child has never been dry), but recent research has cast doubt on this.[11]

We are not sure how to interpret all these findings; they do not necessarily imply that stress and emotional problems *cause* bedwetting, more likely that children may have a biological predisposition to wet the bed which stress can exacerbate, and which in turn causes them and their families distress and stigma so that emotional problems increase. In any event the most important thing for the parent of the bedwetting child to know is that this common problem can be successfully treated in nearly all cases by a simple method (the bell and pad treatment), that such treatment will bring them practical relief and that, if they do seek treatment (initially from their GP who may well refer them to a specialist clinic), their child will almost certainly be a happier person.

Faecal soiling is something else which should always be investigated in any child over four. Again it can have many causes, some physical and some emotional; it is more common than many parents might think (some two per cent of seven- and eight-year-old boys regularly soiled their pants, one survey found,[13] and one per cent of ten-to-twelve-year olds)[14]. It has stronger associations with generalized emotional disorder than enuresis, with which it is often associated.[15]

If either soiling or bedwetting does have a 'meaning' for the child in terms of communicating feelings, explanations favoured by psychodynamically oriented theorists include the suggestion that they are a way of expressing hostility in a child who has difficulty in showing aggression in more direct ways, or that they express a wish to remain a baby and be physically cared for, or that in boys they are an expression of a developing sexuality. Soiling in particular often seems to be one way in which the child asserts her independence in a coercive battle between parents and child; sometimes in young children it is thought to relate to confusions about pregnancy and how babies are made, the child holding on to her motions in imitation of pregnancy. More generally, both soiling and wetting can communicate symbolically the child's inner feelings of 'being in a mess'.

Rituals and obsessions

Rituals and obsessions in a mild form are a normal part of a child's development: preschool children commonly insist on elaborate routines at bedtimes or for dressing or ask for the same questions to be answered over and over again; older children have to avoid or step on the cracks between paving stones, touch certain objects in sequence on their way to school; their games, chants and songs often have a ritualistic quality just as their periodic crazes become almost obsessions.[16] Through these rituals, preoccupations and routines, it is thought, children experiment with taking control over their environment; when for most of the time they are largely subject to control from other people, they can derive great pleasure from sometimes making sure things are done *their* way. As long as parents don't let them take over altogether and can say 'enough' when the fourteenth cuddly toy has had its goodnight kiss, all will be well. Only rituals which are so disruptive that they get in the way of ordinary life are cause for concern; examples might be handwashing that must be done over and over again, schoolwork that must be checked repeatedly. These are, however, relatively uncommon and are associated with other kinds of emotional disorder in the child, with a high incidence of obsessions in the parents themselves in a home that emphasizes etiquette, cleanliness and morality.[17] The obsessional child herself is thought to be experiencing quite a lot of hostility, ambivalence and consequent guilt in her feelings about her parents; she would certainly need professional help.

Eating problems

Extreme food fads (of the fish fingers only variety) are very common in preschool children; they were reported in thirteen per cent of one sample of London three-year-olds.[2] Nearly half of the mothers in the Newsons' Nottingham Study were mildly or very concerned about the amount their child ate. Eating problems in young children are unlikely to be signs of disturbance, although eating at any age can be the setting for disputes between parent and child over issues of independence and control. Whether *over*eating and obesity in childhood are signs of emotional problems is still disputed; anorexia and bulimia nervosa, however, are generally agreed to be symptoms of a psychiatric illness. Interpretation of the symbolic meaning of anorexia symptoms refers to the young girl's wish to avoid the conflicts of growing up, especially issues of sexuality and independence.[18]

Clinging and shyness

Most children under three would rather be with a parent at all times than not with one; reluctance to 'separate' is a normal feature of childhood and is a problem only in so far as most parents are inadequately prepared for the extent of normal clinginess, or for the length of time it will last. With a second child, parents are no longer surprised when she cries if they go upstairs or into the toilet. With the first child such behaviour can seem inexplicable and more than a little burdensome; after the discovery of the child's power it comes as the second great shock of parenthood.

Theories about the development of 'attachment', like that of Dr John Bowlby,[19] help to explain the evolutionary importance of the child's staying close to her mother, and the subtle and delicate system of checks, balances and controls by which the infant maintains that proximity. Observations, such as those of Rheingold and Eckerman,[20] that a one-year-old will on average stray seven metres from its mother in a new place, while a two-year-old strays fifteen metres, a three-year-old seventeen metres and a four-year-old twenty-one metres, show how the child only gradually extends the metaphorical umbilical cord. Such research also shows how, when she is tired, upset or ill, there is a decrease in the physical distance between a child and her attachment figure which she can comfortably tolerate.

It is, then, normal for young children to cling, to cry if left, to be a little angry with the parent when he or she returns after a separation, and to become even more clingy on these occasions. Increased clinginess when the child is tired, ill or upset will persist into the school years but in general, by the time they are four, children are no longer dependent on physical proximity – although fear of *losing* attachment figures lasts right through childhood, as does the need for other kinds of closeness to the parent.

Shyness, or wariness of strangers, first appears around four to six months and is followed in most infants by a normal phase of outright fear of strangers at nine to twelve months. Later shyness may be simply a facet of an introverted rather than extrovert temperament, or an effect of the way the parent labels the child (see chapter 15), or part of a more general fearfulness and difficulty in making any friends. In this latter case it can be a sign that all is not well in the child's life.

Stealing, lying and bullying

Stealing, lying, bullying and other antisocial behaviour problems like wandering or fire-setting can be seen partly as learned behaviours, but partly too as reactions to overwhelming anxieties generated by home environments which are often grossly disadvantaged or disordered.

Stealing by itself need not be quite so serious; it is common (occurring in five per cent of primary school children[21] and, by their own report, in the vast majority of teenage boys)[22]. Children steal for many different reasons, from the young child who has not yet developed concepts of mine and thine to the older child imitating a friend. Psychological studies have outlined several of these types of stealing:[23] unplanned or semiplanned stealing in groups of boys who may not be emotionally disturbed but come from deprived backgrounds lacking in consistent discipline, serious delinquent stealing in older teenagers, and 'comfort stealing' – stealing which often starts at home in early childhood and occurs in unhappy isolated children with a background of rejection by or separation from parents.

Sula Wolff, an eminent Edinburgh psychiatrist, describes the 'comfort stealers' she has met in more detail,[24] noting that a feeling of being unloved by parents often lies behind their acts. She relates how comfort stealing is often seen in children who have lost a mother or are perhaps trying to be accepted by a new step-parent. Others have spoken of the child's attempt to 'recover' the mother, or take from her what he feels he has lacked, in stealing – particularly stealing that occurs inside rather than outside the home.

Lying follows one of two patterns, lying to avoid punishment, or the kind of lie which reflects the child's fantasy and is often a way in which she makes up for low self-esteem. Such 'lies' are rarely told to parents, but to people outside the family; they do give a direct access to the child's inner world and the problems he or she is experiencing – as in the adopted teenage boy who told elaborate tales about a dead younger brother whom he had never had, but whom he would like to have had in the ideal family which he felt had rejected him.

Bullying has been less widely investigated by researchers than other kinds of antisocial behaviour; a recent study in Sweden,[25] however, suggests that there may be little truth in the old stereotype of the bully as an unpopular child, an academic failure who makes up for low self-esteem by exerting power over the weak. Bullies in this study had on the whole a good opinion of themselves, average school attainment and plenty of friends. They differed from non-bullies in being physically stronger and having positive attitudes to violence, with a lack of empathy for others' feelings, and poor relationships with their parents. Boys who were on the receiving end of bullying were not obvious scapegoats in the sense of being noticeably different from other boys (fat, or foreign, or physically handicapped) but they were physically weak, anxious boys with few friends and a close relationship with overprotective, cotton-woolling parents.

Poor concentration and overactivity

The literature on overactive, inattentive and impulsive behaviour is vast, and any detailed discussion is beyond the scope of this book; parents who suspect their child is hyperactive are referred to Eric Taylor's recent book on the subject,[26] and to the discussion in the invaluable *Coping with Young Children* by Jo Douglas and Naomi Richman.[27] For present purposes the question is whether hyperactive behaviour and poor concentration are ways in which a child communicates internal problems, or whether they are purely a consequence of neurological dysfunction, food allergy, genetics, exposure to atmospheric lead pollution or any of the other causative factors which have been proposed at one time or another.

In so far as hyperactivity is often accompanied by aggressive or generally difficult behaviour it may be associated with permissive, weak parental control and with family discord. But 'pure' hyperactivity seems to be different; here the only reliable indicators we have of possible psychological causes are the finding that children who spend their early years in institutions are restless and inattentive at school (and remain so even if adopted into a family),[28] and that there is a high rate of depressive feelings in mothers of hyperactive children.[29] Both these findings are open to several alternative interpretations, however, and all we can conclude is that, if hyperactivity is a response to stress, then the stressors are likely to be long-term ones; there is little evidence that it commonly follows more immediate stressful events such as divorce, bereavement, the birth of a sibling or a hospitalization.

Depression and lethargy

Depression does occur in children as a reaction to recent stresses (particularly the loss of a parent through death or divorce), but it is much less common than in adults and only rarely includes the disturbances of sleep and appetite, the lethargy and loss of interest in life, the impairment in the ability to concentrate and the feelings of guilt and self-blame which characterize adult depression. The child simply feels miserable. Such feelings are quite common (reported by some twelve per cent of ten-year-olds in a large-scale study in the Isle of Wight);[14] it is open to dispute whether they represent the ordinary sadness that is part of life, or whether they should be seen as abnormal. Children cannot perhaps expect or be expected to be happy all the time. It is clear, however, that a child who shows any of the features of adult depression (sudden loss of interest in normal pursuits, a noticeable fall-off in school work, loss of appetite and so on) needs psychological help. Lethargy would be one such feature in the pre-adolescent child, but in adolescence rapid physical growth and bodily changes may bring about a loss of energy (lying in bed all morning, lolling about all day) which, though infuriating, is quite normal.

Tics and stuttering

Tics, such as eye-blinking, head-jerking or repetitive throat-clearing, appear quite often in childhood: between ten and twenty-five per cent will have a tic at some time or other, though most are transient.[30] They do seem to be associated with emotional problems and family stress; they are exacerbated by fatigue, excitement and anxiety. Stuttering, although popularly regarded as an expression of a nervous temperament, is not closely related to emotional disorder and is known to run in families. A pronounced hesitancy in speech is common between the ages of two and four, when the child is trying to frame complex ideas in language which she has not yet quite mastered; parents should avoid calling such a hesitancy a stammer and avoid correcting or calling the child's attention to it, since this in itself can perpetuate what need not become a problem.[16]

Problems of adolescence

Adolescence is a time of change, and a time when parents have a particular need to know what kind of behaviour is 'normal' and what is not. Research by Professor Michael Rutter and his associates in the Isle of Wight has provided us with this kind of information.[31] Their research has shown that 'inner turmoil' (feelings of misery and self-depreciation) is very common in teenagers – more so than in adults. Nearly half of the fourteen-year-olds studied reported that at times they felt so miserable they cried or wanted to get away from everyone and everything. A quarter sometimes felt people were looking at or talking about or laughing at them. One in five felt that they didn't matter very much. But though moody, miserable behaviour is common, another popular stereotype of the teenage years – a breakdown in parent–child relationships – is *not*. The majority of adolescents, it was found, get on well with their parents and continue to be strongly influenced by their values; very few withdraw from family activities or express rejection of their parents. There are family arguments, of course, but they are generally fairly minor. Serious rifts and a sense of alienation between parent and child should not just be accepted as part of growing up in adolescence; they have in all probability begun long before and may be a sign that all is not well in the family.

References

1 K. E. Roberts and J. A. Schoelkopf, 'Eating, sleeping and elimination practices in a group of two-and-a-half-year-old children', *Amer. J. Dis. Childhood*, 82 (1951), 121.

2 N. Richman, J. Stevenson and P. Graham, 'Prevalence of behaviour problems in three-year-old children', *J. Child Psychol. Psychiatry*, 16 (1975), 272–87.

3 J. Dunn and C. Kendrick, *Siblings: Love, Envy and Understanding*, Cambridge, Massachusetts, Harvard University Press, 1982.

4 A. Thomas, S. Chess, H. G. Birch, M. E. Hertzig and S. Korn, *Behavioural Individuality in Early Childhood*, New York University Press, 1963.

5 J. Douglas and N. Richman, *My Child Won't Sleep*, Harmondsworth, Penguin Books, 1984.

6 N. Richman, J. E. Stevenson and P. J. Graham, *Preschool to School: A Behavioural Study*, London, Academic Press, 1982.

7 H. Gastaut and R. J. Broughton, 'A clinical and polygraphic study of episodic phenomena during sleep', in J. Wortis (ed.), *Recent Advances in Biological Psychiatry*, New York, Plenum Press, 1965.

8 J. Dunn, 'Feeding and sleeping', in M. Rutter (ed.), *Scientific Foundations of Developmental Psychiatry*, London, Heinemann Medical Books, 1980.

9 D. Schaffer, 'The development of bladder control', in M. Rutter (ed.), *Scientific Foundations of Developmental Psychiatry*, London, Heinemann Medical Books, 1980.

10 H. Bakwin, 'Enuresis in children', *J. Ped.*, 58 (1961), 806–19.

11 D. Schaffer, 'Enuresis' in M. Rutter and L. Hersov (eds.), *Child and Adolescent Psychiatry*, 2nd edn., Oxford, Blackwell Scientific Publications, 1985.

12 J. W. B. Douglas, 'Early disturbing events and later enuresis', in J. Kolvin, R.

MacKeith and S. R. Meadow (eds.), *Bladder Control and Enuresis*, Clinics in Developmental Medicine, Nos. 48/49, London, Heinemann/SIMP, 1973.

13 M. Bellman, 'Studies in encopresis', *Acta Paediat. Scand.*, Suppl. 170 (1966).

14 M. Rutter, J. Tizard and K. Whitmore (eds.), *Education, Health and Behaviour*, London, Longman, 1970.

15 L. Hersov, 'Faecal soiling', in M. Rutter and L. Hersov (eds.), *Child and Adolescent Psychiatry*, 2nd edn., Oxford, Blackwell Scientific Publications, 1985.

16 S. Wolff, *Children under Stress*, 2nd edn., Harmondsworth, Penguin, 1973.

17 P. L. Adams, *Obsessive Children: A Sociopsychiatric Study*, London, Butterworth, 1973.

18 A. H. Crisp, *Let me Be*, London, Academic Press, 1980.

19 J. Bowlby, *Attachment and Loss:* vol. I: *Attachment*, 2nd edn., New York, Basic Books, 1982.

20 H. L. Rheingold and C. O. Eckerman, 'Fear of the stranger: a critical examination', in H. W. Reese (ed.), *Advances in Child Development and Behaviour*, vol. 8, New York, Academic Press, 1973.

21 S. Wolff, 'Behavioural characteristics of primary school children referred to a psychiatric department', *Brit J. Psychiatry*, 113 (1967), 885–93.

22 D. J. West, *The Young Offender*, Harmondsworth, Penguin, 1967.

23 J. Rich, 'Types of stealing', *Lancet* I (1956), 496–8.

24 S. Wolff, 'Nondelinquent disturbances of conduct' in M. Rutter and L. Hersov (eds.), *Child and Adolescent Psychiatry: Modern Approaches*, 2nd edn., Oxford, Blackwell Scientific Publications, 1985.

25 D. Olweus, 'Bullies and the bullied', in N. Frude and H. Gault (eds.), *Disruptive Behaviour in Schools*, London, Wiley, 1984.

26 E. Taylor, *The Hyperactive Child: A Parent's Guide*, London, Martin Dunitz, 1985.

27 J. Douglas and N. Richman, *Coping with Young Children*, Harmondsworth, Penguin Books, 1984.

28 B. Tizard and J. Hodges, 'The effect of early institutional rearing on the development of eight-year-old children, *J. Child Psychol. Psychiatry*, 19 (1978), 99–118.

29 S. Sandberg, M. Wieselberg and D. Schaffer, 'Hyperkinetic and conduct–problem children in a primary school population: some epidemiological considerations', *J. Child Psychol. Psychiatry*, 21 (1980), 293–311.

30 J. A. Corbett and G. Turpin, 'Tics and Tourette's syndrome', in M. Rutter and L. Hersov (eds.), *Child and Adolescent Psychiatry: Modern Approaches*, 2nd edn., Oxford, Blackwell Scientific Publications, 1985.

31 M. Rutter, P. Graham, O. Chadwick and W. Yule, 'Adolescent turmoil: fact or fiction?', *J. Child Psychol. Psychiatry*, 17 (1976), 35–56.

9 Communication II

If a child is showing any of the problem behaviours we have just discussed, or more simply a general emotional malaise, and the parent wants to find out why, the first place to look might be recent events in his life and potential sources of stress. Second, the parent would want to bear in mind the concerns which are likely to be foremost in the child's mind at his particular age and stage. Third, he or she might need skills – some of them unfamiliar and outside the range of everyday parenting – which would help him or her to talk over problems and feelings with the child. In this chapter we will look in turn at each of these three issues.

Stress in childhood

Children are indeed subject to stress, just as adults are, and seem to react to it in a similar way. There is a long list of events which have been shown to impose acute or chronic stress on them: hospitalization (particularly between the ages of six months and four years), parental conflict, divorce, the birth of siblings, school entry, bereavement, illness in the family, school failure. There are also less obvious stressors, the ordinary life events which mean *change* (sometimes even change for the better, such as holidays, Christmas, a new friendship, joining a club): research with children has shown that scores based on the number of such life events in a given period predicts, as with adults, the likelihood that the child will experience subsequent psychological disturbance or physical illness.[1] For example, in one study families were asked to keep a diary of upsetting events; the number of such events was clearly related to the likelihood of the child developing a sore throat or other upper respiratory tract infection over the next two weeks.[2] Another study[3] found that a high life-event score predicted the child's liability to accident of any kind. If they know that their child has been through a period of upheaval and change, parents need to be prepared for his reaction, either emotional or physical.

They cannot, of course, protect their children from all stress, nor should they: there is some evidence that the experience of coping successfully with mild stresses can inoculate or protect the child against later upsets.[4] The crucial issue appears to be whether the stress experience leaves the child with a feeling of 'I can cope, because I did before', or whether it has been too great and has simply overwhelmed him. If the stress is too great it may actually *increase* his future vulnerability: a week away from his parents at the age of two might well make him much less able to cope with a few days in hospital a year or two later, while a series of carefully planned short afternoon play sessions with a friend while his mother goes out shopping might have the opposite effect.

How to foster the 'I can cope' feeling in children is something we know too little about; for the older child, teaching relaxation techniques to handle anxiety (see chapter 11) may well be helpful; for children of all ages parents can try to teach problem-solving techniques[5] – that is, when their child is faced with a potentially stressful situation, they should help him to think of things *he* can do about it, rather than try to sort things out for him ('Why do you think May has said she's not your friend any more? Can you think of any other reasons? How can you react? Can you think of other ways? What would happen if you –? What will you try first?'). Reinforcing successful coping with praise ('I thought you handled that really well') is also likely to be important.

The child's concerns

Stress is only rarely universal; what will bother one child will not necessarily bother another. All parents know that the child's temperament, sex, history and age will affect his reactions, so that their sociable, happy-go-lucky son can cope with a change of school, whereas their quieter daughter with her one close friend would find a change difficult. Each child will view a new event in terms of his own personal concerns.

While many of these concerns are purely individual, some can be understood in broad age and stage terms. A knowledge of how these ages and stages have been conceptualized in the psychological literature (in particular, by the highly influential E. H. Erikson,[6] and more recently by Sula Wolff)[7] can be of real help to the parent in his effort to understand and communicate with the child.

The infant begins life, Erikson suggests, with a basic experience of dependency, a basic relationship of himself and one other person (the 'maternal person'), and a basic learned outcome of either a sense of trust or mistrust in the ability of the world outside to take care of him. His concerns, if he can be said to have concerns at his age, are mainly about the reliability with which his needs will be met.

In the next phase, when he is a toddler, he develops several new concerns. The relationship he now needs to handle is a three-person one; parents who previously made no demands on him now begin to ask that he behave in certain ways, do this and not do that; the issue between them and the child is one of compliance, and the child's concern is to assert his will and his independence, against a background of continuing strong need for both physical and emotional closeness to those he loves. This is the 'no' stage, closely followed by 'I want mummy'. Ambivalence between dependence and independence is much in evidence. The outcome of this stage, if all goes well, is a sense of autonomy. But on the way to autonomy, there are many frustrations – frustrations because the child cannot manage to do certain things yet, or because he is not allowed to – and the frustrations can lead to tantrums and aggression. Separations, even brief, can provoke distress and protest. The child's 'problem' behaviour can be a natural consequence of his urgent concerns.

Between the ages of three and five many children have to learn to cope with a rival for their parents' attention and affection, in the shape of a brother or sister: the three-person situation broadens to become 'the family'. The concerns of this age group are to do with their place in the family, their own worth in the sense both of competence and continuing love-worthiness, their embryonic sense of self. Questions (who am I like? mummy? daddy?) begin to be asked as the child learns to identify with one or other parent and to begin to compare himself with others. Partly through identification, he develops a conscience and begins to feel guilt and anxiety as a result of real or imagined wrongdoings. Sometimes apparently inexplicable fears and worries at this age can be the result of such imagined badness and the punishment the child fears it will bring.

At five or six the world widens to include school, the challenges of learning or not learning, and the all-important peer group. The child has to learn what kind of person he is outside the protective perspective of his own family. His concerns are now about his own abilities or lack of them – he needs to feel good about himself and may not always be able to – and his acceptability to other children. At first he needs 'a friend' – anyone will do, so long as he has one. Later he has to learn about groups. Sula Wolff observes how children between six and ten seem to be practising how to establish and maintain social groups, learning how to prop up their self-esteem by belonging to such a group or tribe, and learning how to conform to the group and keep away 'outsiders' – those unfortunate outsiders who are teased because they are in some small way different from the norms of the group. The careless cruelty of children in this age group, their name-calling, the games in which someone is 'out' are all, Dr Wolff suggests, manifest-ations of this process of learning to belong. Conversely, the worries and problems of this stage will be about *not* belonging. The child who has to have extra help with reading at school will be upset not so much because he sees himself as a failure but because he will *be seen* to be one every time he has to leave his class to go to the special teacher: it is the public admission of differentness which will hurt him most. The greatest need to conform in dress and tastes is found in this age group; not, as was once thought, in adolescence, but in the immediate pre-adolescent years. Parents may not care very much for such slavish conformity, or for the persecution of outsiders, but they will have to respect it.

The concerns of the adolescent continue for a while on the lines of in-groups and out-groups, fashions and fads. But, if for the infant there is the experience of dependency and the acquisition of a basic sense of trust, if for the toddler there is learning how to handle battles of will between himself and those who make the rules for him, if for the pre-school child there is coping with the need to share love within the family, if for the school-age child there is how to get on in a group, then for the teenager there is the basic learning task of how to break free, become truly independent and establish a unique identity. In order to disengage himself, he may need to rebel: he rationalizes the loosening of strong bonds by turning for a short while against the very people he cares for most, who for so long have been at the centre of his life. He becomes hypercritical; he can't stand the way they talk or dress or think, and everything they do is wrong in his eyes. As he tries to let go of his family, he has the task of putting something in place of the security and stable values it offers. That something is a secure sense of self, of what *he* is – what he thinks, feels, believes in. Hence the question most teenagers seem to be asking themselves much of the time: who am I? Hence their need to experiment with different rules, to posture, assert themselves and flaunt whatever aspect of identity they are currently trying out. Hence too the sense of loss which they feel when they cut the emotional ties which have held them, a loss and emptiness which they will fill with temporary heroes, political and social ideals, religious fervour.

Some psychologists believe that as well as the new tasks of establishing identity and letting go of the family, adolescence brings a reawakening of unresolved conflicts from the learning stages of earlier years and perhaps a second chance to solve them. Some of the strange ways in which adolescents behave can profitably be seen in this light – for example, their infantile, passive dependency one minute, their rebellious negativism the next, their sulky shyness, their insistence on creating and leaving a mess wherever they go, the capacity for idealization and their need to replace those fallen idols of early childhood, the parents. All these may well remind the parent of stages they thought were long ago left behind. Certainly parents need to be aware of how the coming of puberty reactivates a particular set of feelings, to do with the triangular mother–father–child relationship of the early years. Much of the traditional mother–daughter and father–son conflict in the teenage period can be put down to this reawakening of rivalries and jealousies within the family group.

Talking with children: listening to feelings

When a parent suspects that the child is having difficulty in managing the developmental tasks of his current stage, or that his basic concerns are being challenged, he will want to help by talking things over. But asking direct questions ('What's wrong?') or proffering direct solutions ('Well, just leave her alone and find another friend') is rarely successful. Often there seems no way to start, although both parties want to communicate; neither can find the way in.

The useful psychological contribution here comes from the work of Carl Rogers,[8] a counsellor and therapist who established what he called non-directive techniques to help clients work through their emotional problems. His first principle was this: that in order to help, the counsellor must listen not just to what the client is saying, but to what he is *feeling*, and that he can open up communication by restating (reflecting) to the client the feelings which lie behind the words.

Consider these conversations:

Child: I've got nothing to do.
Parent: What do you mean you've got nothing to do? You've a cupboard full of toys and . . .

Child: You gave Mary more sweets than me [Mary is his sister].
Parent: No, I didn't – look, you've got five sweets same as her.

Child: I can't do it.
Parent: Of course you can if you try.

In all these exchanges the parent has responded to the child's words strictly on a reality level. He has used the language of facts but not the language of feeling. Something very different is happening here:

Child: I've got nothing to do.
Parent: You're really feeling bored today, aren't you? Perhaps you're wanting to ask if I will spend some time with you.

Child: You gave Mary more sweets than me.
Parent: Sometimes you're afraid your sister might get more from me than you do.

Child: I can't do it.
Parent: It seems difficult and hard work to you, doesn't it?

What the parent has done in these exchanges is to take a guess, the best guess available to him, at the child's feelings. He has shown the child that he understands, or at least is trying to understand, those feelings, and that he accepts the reality of those feelings, whether they be good or bad. Something has threatened the child's basic concerns, so that he feels jealous, incompetent, left out of the group or whatever. Someone else – the parent – has let him know that he has a right to feel that way. From that point effective communication becomes possible.

Showing that we understand a child's feelings does not mean trying to jolly him out of them or smooth things over. This is seldom useful. Most adults have had times when they have felt mildly depressed and have experienced comments from friends such as 'Cheer up', 'count your blessings, things will soon get better'. They know this already, and it doesn't help; at the moment of depression the best thing a friend can say is something like 'I'm sorry you're feeling so low; everything must be looking very black to you right now.'

So it is with children. If your child had to miss a swimming lesson at school because of an ear infection, he does not want to hear you say 'Never mind; I'm sure some other children missed it too and next week you'll be able to go, and what's one time?' He would certainly prefer you to convey that you know just how bad he felt watching other people swim when he couldn't. Another example: if you have to move house, the temptation is to point out to the child all the good things about the move, the things he'll be able to do, the nice new school. 'You'll soon make new friends' is what most parents would say. It is better, however, to use words like 'I know you'll miss your friends here; it is sad to lose people.' Children, like adults, must be allowed to experience (and get over) the bad feelings, anger and sadness, as well as the good ones. Constantly reassuring the child may be a way in which the parent avoids having to share the child's painful feelings: no one likes to see the child unhappy, even if the unhappiness is only temporary. But though reassurance is temporarily soothing and consoling, it does not give the child the chance to work through his problems.

Some of the things a child feels may make the parent so uncomfortable that he or she needs to reject them altogether and deny what the child is trying to express. These are some common exchanges involving denial, along with alternative ways of reacting:

Child: I hate school.
Parent: Don't be so silly – you know you love it really.
or
Parent: There are some things about school that really bother you.

Child: I hate *you.*
Parent: Don't you talk to me like that.
or
Parent: Sometimes you feel angry with me.

The alternatives allow the child to say more about what it is that bothers him or makes him angry; the denial closes the conversation and will make the child reluctant to express his feelings again. Why should he, when no one believes or wants to hear him? The problem is that if he is not allowed to express them directly, they will find other, harder-to-handle, ways of surfacing – daily stomach-aches before school, for example, or aggression displaced to peers or siblings or teachers.

Sometimes the parent needs to listen not only to the feelings behind words, but to the ways in which the child is using actions, questions, even drawings to symbolize his feelings. The temporary obsessions which some children develop are especially worth 'listening' to:

> John, aged six, was a highly intelligent, restless, tense little boy who had recently been through a period of upheaval in which his parents separated, his mother left for another country, and his father planned also to move to a new job overseas. For a few weeks he showed a great interest in learning about whirlwinds, cyclones and tornadoes; he would recite over and over again, in a kind of chant, the properties of a tornado – 'a tornado moves at 250 mph and is extremely dangerous'. He drew tornadoes, storms, 'a man floating in space with nothing to hold on to'. He needed at that point someone to let him know that his own feeling of being lost in a storm which he did not understand, and which sometimes he feared he had helped to create, was understood; he needed someone to suggest 'Perhaps sometimes you feel a bit like that man with nothing to hold on to.'

> Elizabeth, aged seven, was shy and anxious, lacking in confidence and doing poorly at school. Her family had been through a very difficult time; when Elizabeth was four her baby sister died (a cot death). After the baby died, Elizabeth began to ask all sorts of strange questions, mainly about whether objects might break or disappear, or whether they could be mended. At night she would go through another routine of questions: 'Will anyone come into the house while I'm asleep? Is anyone under the bed? Will anyone hurt me?' No amount of reassurance stopped her asking these same questions over and over again. The questions were her way of expressing a feeling that the world was no longer a trustworthy place; as a first step her parents needed to put that feeling into words for her – 'Since Joanne died, it seems to you that none of us are safe any more.'

Talking with a child: aids to communication

Reflecting feelings is one way of opening up communication with a child without asking him directly what is on his mind: if he comes in, slams the front door and throws his schoolbag on the floor, the parent who says 'Feeling fed up?' will get further than the one who says 'Whatever's the matter with *you*?' But there are, in addition to reflecting feelings, some particular ways of starting off a conversation that are sometimes useful. At bedtime the parent can make a sort of game and ask 'What did you like about today?' After the child has answered, the parent tells what he/she liked. Then he can ask 'What did you not like?' and respond in some way which suggests acceptance and understanding of the child's feelings, while not trying to explain away whatever it was the child disliked. Other games might be 'Something you like about yourself . . . something you don't like about yourself', 'Something you are looking forward to tomorrow . . . something you aren't looking forward to', 'Something you did today which you felt good about . . . something you did today which you felt bad about'.[10] For young children dolls and soft toys are invaluable aids to communication. The parents might pick up teddy and remark that 'He looks a bit sad, wonder what's been happening to him today?'

Family communication: 'I' messages

Listening to feelings and problems is only half of effective communication. The other half is the ability to express one's own feelings in an open and straightforward way. Children can be helped to recognize, label and communicate feelings only if they have adult models to imitate: parents who are able, for example, in the conversation about moving house to add 'I don't much like the idea of moving either, and I'm certainly going to miss my friends a lot', or who, on a bad morning when everything seems to be going wrong, can tell their children 'I'm in a really bad mood, that's why I yelled at you – it was nothing you've done.'

These 'I' messages, as some psychologists call them,[9] are a very useful way of improving communication in families and can be learned by both parents and children: when a teenager persists in leaving his clothes all over the floor, for example, the 'I' message the parent should practise would be 'When you leave all your clothes on the floor, I feel angry. I feel furious', rather than the accusatory 'you' message 'You're a real slob; why do you have to be so messy?' Similarly, when a husband arrives home late from work, there is the 'I' message 'When you are late I feel really worried, in case something has happened to you', which is more likely to be effective than 'You're late again! You're so thoughtless.'

Unsuccessful family communication

Like unsuccessful parenting, unsuccessful family communication patterns have been the focus of much psychological research: the aim has been to discover how members of families with a disturbed or difficult child habitually communicate with one another – or fail to. One of the most important findings, from the point of view of parents, is that in such families messages often lack clarity and accuracy; there is a mismatch between what the parent says to the child and what he really means.[11] At the extreme, this could be the parent who says 'Come here and sit near me', while his tone of voice, his facial expression and his posture express coldness and rejection. More commonly, there are messages like 'You don't want to do that', when the parent ought to be saying 'You want to do that but I'm not going to let you', or commands masquerading as questions – 'Do you want to go to bed?' – when the message is really 'It's your bedtime.'

Dishonest communication with children – trickery, bending of the truth – is also common, more so than we often realize:[12] it might range from telling a child that the doctor brought the new baby to false threats ('The policeman will come for you if you do that') or outright lies ('I'll be back before you know it') when leaving the child with a babysitter for a whole morning. Such distorted communication may make adults feel better, but it will not help the child. The child needs messages that are at all times straightforward, clear and honest.

Communication and the self-concept

One final aspect of communication which parents need to know about concerns the possible effects, for good or bad, of the things they say *about* their children. In most families children come to attract labels: the shy one, the clever one, the naughty one, the worrier, the clumsy one, the bossy one. Parents notice their children's different temperamental characteristics and seek to explain their behaviour (and render it more predictable) by attaching these labels. The child turns away from the stranger, and the parent apologizes: 'He's always been shy.' The child is doing badly at school, and the parent tells the teachers 'He never could concentrate.' Most of the time the child is there to hear what is said about him, and there to add it to his developing picture of himself – his self-concept.

The problem comes when he not only adds a label to his self-concept but starts to live up to it. There is increasing evidence that the way children think of themselves affects the way they behave; that if, for instance, they are told they are shy they will go on being shy,[13] that if they think they are stupid, they will act stupid. This was demonstrated in a fascinating experiment by Robert Hartley in a London primary school:[14] he showed that children from disadvantaged home backgrounds who normally made many mistakes when matching complex shapes could be induced to reduce their error rate dramatically simply by being told to 'act like someone clever' when tackling the task.

That a child might wish to live up to a *positive* concept of himself is easy to understand; the reasons why he lives up to negative labels are more complex. Research in the field of social psychology does, however, suggest how it could come about. Such research has shown that adults and children have a strong in-built motivation to hang on to attitudes they hold and will actively seek out information that confirms these attitudes, while rejecting information that doesn't fit in with them. Many psychological experiments have demonstrated how, for example, heavy smokers, given a newspaper to read and later asked to recall articles in it about smoking, will recall only the articles suggesting the health risks of smoking have been exaggerated. Reading or hearing things that don't fit in with pre-existing attitudes makes us psychologically uncomfortable – even if the attitudes we hold are unproductive or outdated. Attitudes to self follow the same rules. A child who has cast himself into a particular role, seeing himself perhaps as 'shy' or 'babyish' or black sheep of the family, will not easily give up the role. For a while he has to risk losing the predictability and sense of control over personal relationships which the role has afforded him. Like the six-year-old who said, when his mother tried to tell him what a good boy he was for something he had done, 'But I'm not a good boy, I'm *bad*', he may prefer the devil he knows to the angel he does not. Unless they want then to be saddled for good with a naughty, shy, scatterbrained or selfish child, the parents should take care not to apply these or any other negative labels to their children.

References

1 R. D. Coddington, 'The significance of life events as etiologic factors in the diseases of children', *J. Psychosom. Res.*, 16 (1972), 205–13.

2 R. J. Meyer and R. J. Haggerty, 'Streptococcal infections in families', *Paediatrics*, 29 (1962), 539–49.

3 E. R. Padilla, D. J. Rohsenow and A. B. Bergman, 'Predicting accident frequency in children', *Paediatrics*, 58 (1976), 223–6.

4 M. Rutter, *Maternal Deprivation Re-assessed*, 2nd edn., Harmondsworth, Penguin Books, 1981.

5 M. B. Shure and G. Spivack, *Problem-Solving Techniques in Child-Rearing*, San Francisco, Jossey-Bass, 1978.

6 E. H. Erikson, *Childhood and Society*, New York, Norton, 1950.

7 S. Wolff, *Children Under Stress*, 2nd edn., Harmondsworth, Penguin Books, 1973.

8 C. Rogers, *On Becoming a Person*, Boston, Houghton-Mifflin, 1961.

9 T. Gordon, *Parent Effectiveness Training*, New York, Wyden, 1970.

10 B. Remsberg and A. Saunders, *Help Your Child Cope with Stress*, London, Piatkus, 1986.

11 D. E. Bugental, L. R. Love, J. W. Kaswan and C. April, 'Verbal–nonverbal conflict in parental messages to normal and disturbed children', *J. Abnorm. Psychol*, 77 (1971), 6–10.

12 J. Newson and E. Newson, *Four Years Old in an Urban Community*, London, Allen and Unwin, 1968.
13 P. C. Zimbardo, *Shyness*, Reading, Massachusetts, Addison-Wesley, 1977.
14 R. Hartley, 'Imagine you're clever', *J. Child Psychol. Psychiatry*, 27 (1986), 383–98.

10 Children thinking

In order that two people communicate, they must be talking about the same thing; the closer the resemblance between the ways in which they each look at a topic, the better will be their communication. But do children and adults see things in the same way? It is this question we now need to address.

Most adults assume that children's thinking is basically similar to that of adults – slower maybe, and less efficient, but still following the same kind of logic. Some of the most fascinating research in child psychology, however, shows that this just isn't so. Children's thought processes are not scaled-down versions of ours, but startlingly different. Not until they reach adolescence do they begin to use the kind of logic adults take for granted as 'thinking'. If we don't understand something of their particular kind of logic, we will often be sending messages they won't follow, expecting unrealistically high standards of behaviour, or failing to understand their fears and worries.

The young child: two to seven

A small girl was watching a crying baby with concern; she went up and stroked the baby, offered him toys, then when these tactics failed, and even though the baby's own mother was there, she went to bring *her own* mother to the rescue.[1]

A little boy, having reduced his mother to tears by his behaviour, went to get his special 'cuddly' (a blanket) and gave it to her to hold.[2]

John, aged three, begged his parents to take him home from hospital, where he was spending a few days for a routine operation: 'Please mummy, please daddy . . . I won't be bad any more,' he said.

Joanna, aged five, was talking with her mother: Joanna: 'Look, my shadow's moving. It's alive.' Mother: 'Well . . . maybe not. When you throw a ball, is the ball alive?' Joanna: 'Yes, it's alive. It can move.'

Peter, aged three and a half, on being asked 'If you wore a dress and played with a doll, would you be a girl or a boy?', answered: 'A girl, of course.'[3]

Children of varying ages were watching an adult placing a number of different coloured counters in a bag, then pulling out one counter at a time. Before every draw, the adult asked the children to predict what colour would be drawn. 'Blue,' said a ten-year-old, 'blue hasn't come up for a while.' 'Red,' said one four-year-old confidently, and when asked why: "Cos I like red."[1]

These examples make it very clear that the young child's logic is not the same as our own. She has some strange ideas about probability, life and gender; she thinks she has been sent to hospital by her parents because she was naughty and the hospital would make her 'better'; she is sure that what works for her when she is sad will work for others too.

We can describe the essential qualities of her thought in several ways, all of which we owe to the celebrated Swiss psychologist Jean Piaget. The first important quality, which every parent should know about, is *egocentricism*: the young child's thought is tied to her own viewpoint, and only her own viewpoint. Piaget, in one experiment,[4] showed children between four and twelve years of age a model of cardboard mountains, which varied in colour, snow cover and other features. The child sat on one side of the mountain scene; a doll was placed on the other side. The child was then asked to choose from a set of pictures 'the one that shows what the doll can see'. Children below six or seven almost always chose for the doll a perspective exactly the same as their own and were perfectly happy with their choice. As far as they were concerned, everyone saw things exactly as they did.

Parents listening to a child describing her first day at school may have great difficulty following her explanations: if they listen hard, they will find that the child is speaking almost *as if they had been there too*, as if they had seen the games she had played with and knew exactly what 'that round thingy' was. Again, the child is not able to put herself in the place of another person and therefore does not understand what they already know, what they don't know and need to be told.

Now much research work has been done on the question of the young child's egocentricity since Piaget's first experiments, and some of his conclusions have been questioned – for example, it has been found that in situations which make practical sense to the child (such as being asked to hide a small boy doll behind cardboard walls so that a policeman doll 'can't see him')[5] even three- and four-year-olds can momentarily adopt a perspective other than their own, and that in particular they can show a very accurate understanding of others' feelings if those others are very familiar to them (as with brothers and sisters).[2] On the whole, however, it does remain useful to say that the young child sees herself at the centre of her world, and that, when she does show awareness of other perspectives, this awareness is fragile and can easily be swept away.

Because of her one-sided perspective, the child often misinterprets her environment – will believe, for example, that, when the moon seems to move in the sky at night, it is actually following her, or that if her parents quarrel she or her behaviour must be the cause.[6] Her parents will often need to explain that some things are not her fault, just as not everything in the world is there for her benefit. They need to tolerate on occasion what may seem like outrageous selfishness; although the 'how would you feel if . . .' line of thought has to be encouraged when one child has hurt another, they should not be surprised if the child finds this idea hard to grasp. They should beware of expectations that a child will be able to understand both sides of an issue – that she will be able to cope in any way at all, for example, with the rapid shifts of perspective involved in shuttling between two battling separated parents, each of whom is criticizing the other.

Along with egocentricism, Piaget described a second quality of the young child's thought which he labelled *animism*. The four-year-old believes that everything is alive and has feelings as she does; if it moves in any way, it is conscious. The stars, the moon, clouds, a teddy bear or favourite doll are all credited by her with wishes and feelings. Even at six she may still say that the sun is alive (although a stone is not: by now she restricts the definition to things that move by themselves without outside agency). Animism is accompanied by a confusion between what is real and what is not real: imaginary things, to the young child, exist outside the imagination and can be seen and shared by others. Three-year-olds in one study in Denmark[7] were shown various real objects and asked to think about others that were not actually in the room ('my tricycle at home') and about figures from fairy tales or comic strips (a giant, Mickey Mouse). The experimenters asked them a series of questions, 'Is it a real bike that you can ride? Could you actually meet Donald Duck in the street and play with him? Would you be able to touch your bike? Can you touch this lamp? Would you be able to touch Mickey Mouse? Is your bike still there when nobody thinks about it? Does a giant exist when nobody thinks of him – or is he only something we play with and imagine?' The three-year-olds showed a pronounced tendency to experience imaginary items as in every respect like real ones; by four they were less likely to do this, and by six the tendency had practically disappeared.

Another question asked in this experiment was whether the child could change real or imaginary things simply by wanting them changed ('Can you make the lamp red if you wish it to turn red? Can you make Donald Duck twice as big simply by thinking about it?'). Again, the youngest children believed they could; they showed what is often call *magical thinking*. They believed that their thoughts and wishes had the power to alter the real world.

Adults too are seen as having enormous and magical powers: the child believes, for example, that if she is ill, her mother could have prevented it if she wished.[6] She thinks, when she is young, that adults must always be right; if psychologists ask her strange questions ('Is milk bigger than water?') she will ponder the problem very solemnly and try to oblige with an answer, while the child over seven will laugh at the question and the silly behaviour of the questioner.[8]

The end point of belief in the infallibility of adults, and the magical powers of people and objects, is a denial that anything in the world happens by accident. To the young child everything that happens is meant to happen; even things like garbage landing on the floor instead of the bin, when thrown, are seen by four-year-olds as intended.

A final feature of the young child's thinking is that it is very much tied to the here and now, and the immediate *look of things*. At this age the child is on the whole much more visual than verbal in the way she thinks, whereas the adult's thinking is dominated by the power of words. If asked, for example, to put a pile of pictures into groups on the basis of 'what goes together',[9] a five-year-old might choose, say, an apple and a house with a red door "Cos they've both got red on them'; the older child groups by function ('These are things you can eat') or superordinate class ('These are all fruit'). Again, as Piaget demonstrated in a long series of very well-known experiments,[4] before the age of six or seven a perceptual change – a change in surface appearances only – is often enough to alter the child's judgement about the number of counters in a row, the volume of liquid in a jar, or the amount of plasticine in a ball. If a row of counters is spread out so that it looks longer, the child will say there are now 'more' counters than in a matching row which has not been spread out. If the child is shown two identically shaped jars each filled with water to the same level, then when water from one is poured into a wide shallow bowl the child will say there is now less to drink in the bowl than in the jar. If she compares two identical balls of plasticine and says they are the same, then watches as one is rolled into a long snake, she may judge that there is now more plasticine in the snake.

These findings by Piaget have been the subject of some controversy, just as have his findings on egocentricism. Others have shown that on some occasions the child can be less dependent on the look of things and can use a more adultlike logic – when the line-of-counters experiment is repeated with a line of Smarties, for example, or if the perceptual transformation is made not by the all-powerful adult but by the child herself or a toy figure like a 'naughty teddy'.[8] The conclusion that psychologists are now reaching is a compromise: that young children can reason logically, but that their ability to do so cannot be relied on.

In practice, the parent will meet many instances of the focus on surface appearances in his or her child. The small boy who in our earlier example judged gender by what someone wore or played with was showing this kind of prelogical thought. For him things are what they look like. And if things are only what they look like, they can very easily be changed. By wearing a dress and playing with a doll, the boy can 'become' a girl. There are no absolutes: the world of the young child is both fluid and uncertain. It can turn on a word or a glance, a thought or a wish.

Adults need to think hard about what it would mean to live in a world where the essence of things changed from moment to moment, according to what they looked like at the time, a world without accidents, a world where dreams and fairy tales were as real or unreal as the rest of one's experience, a world where wishes (both good and bad) could come true. Such a world would surely be a frightening place as well as an exciting one. It is so far from our own logical, ordered and predictable experience that we forget what it was like, just as we forget our dreams: neither are compatible with the way we usually think, and we have no slots in our mental filing system from which to retrieve them.

The potential for *confusion* in the young child is enormous: this above all is what the parent, trying to put himself or herself in the child's place, must remember. If we look again at Elizabeth, whose distress when her baby sister died was described in chapter 9, we can see some of these confusions in action:

> Like all young children, Elizabeth had seen her parents as all powerful. They had always before been able to protect her, to mend things that were broken. But then the baby died: why couldn't they mend the baby too? Why did they let it happen? Most important, was it her own occasional angry, jealous feelings towards the baby that had made it happen? She had sometimes wished the baby wasn't there, and now it wasn't. There would be punishment, someone would come to punish her and she could never feel safe.

Elizabeth's family went through an extreme event; fortunately few children have to face what she faced. Nevertheless any child can imagine, in her egocentric and magical way, that she caused even minor illness or accident to loved ones; any child can think an adult has deliberately let her down when nothing of the sort was intended; any child can fear she will be sent away because in a moment's anger a parent has said 'I've had enough of you.' Sometimes, when children are young, parenthood means explaining the things we do not see as needing an explanation; it means a very great effort to understand what could be going on in the child's mind; it means taking extreme care with what we say or imply to them.

Middle childhood and adolescence

We do not need to take quite so much care with the older child; her thinking is more robust and she is less likely to misinterpret meanings. Psychologists like Piaget still, however, have insights to offer the parent on what to expect and how to explain things in the middle years of childhood. In this period there are still limitations on the child's thought processes: the main limitation is that, until she becomes a teenager, she is still only able to reason logically about real, concrete experiences. She does not think in the abstract, but the here and now. If you ask her if, on the whole, she is a 'happy' person she might tell you 'Yes' because she went swimming that day, or 'No' because no one played with her at break, but she will not grasp the idea of happiness as an abstract or long-term quality. She reasons always from the concrete to the general, and not the other way round as we do. Ask her to play twenty questions: whereas an adult or teenager will generate large-scale hypotheses and ask questions like 'Is it an animal? Can you eat it?', the younger child will go straight into concrete guesses like 'Is it a dog? Is it bread?'

Good primary school teachers are aware of the child's tendency to reason from the particular to the general and use teaching methods which start from concrete, immediate experiences: rather than presenting a lesson on 'Life on the seashore' they would begin with the seashell the child brought into school and have her sketch it, write about it and use books to find out more about the creature it once held. Parents are in an excellent position to help their child's educational and cognitive development like this. They can also help the child's emotional development by remembering to put explanations of potentially upsetting events into concrete form – a good example being time concepts, where instead of saying 'Daddy will be away on business for a fortnight', they could mark on a wall calendar the fourteen days and have the child cross off each day as it passes. Again, if a friend is moving away from the area, the child needs not just to know where the friend is going and to look at a map, but also to be told how far that is in relation to other familiar journeys – 'as far as granny's'. If the parent is trying to point out to the child the consequences of her actions, they must be expressed as real events and not just hypothetical abstractions. When the child becomes an adolescent, she will begin to inhabit the world of the possible as well as the actual, and she will actively experiment with ideals and abstract notions – to imagine what it might have been like, for example, *if* she had been born to poverty, so that she develops a wish to help others. But until she reaches this stage her parents have to attend to her need for real experience in acquiring meanings for events.

The child's concept of right and wrong

Children's thinking about right and wrong is a particularly good example both of the way in which their logic develops, and of the way in which in the earlier stages it differs from our own. Young children up to the age of seven or eight view acts only by their consequences – thinking, for example, a boy who broke a window accidentally while playing football deserved a greater punishment than a boy who had deliberately kicked a football into a puddle so that it splashed a passer-by. It is the scale of the damage that matters to them, not the intentions behind events. Similarly, they judge the seriousness of a lie by how much it bends the truth, not by whether there is an intention to deceive:[10] they would say it was *not* naughty to tell your family you got good marks in school if you didn't, because it often does happen that you get good marks, whereas it *was* naughty to say, after being frightened by a dog, that it was as big as a horse – because a dog simply could not ever be that size. Moreover, it would not be naughty to say you got good marks if you were believed: to be naughty means to be punished and, if you are not punished, you cannot have been naughty.

If you have been naughty, on the other hand, the young child believes you will always be punished. An example of this belief comes from another of Jean Piaget's studies,[11] in which children were told the following story:

> The teacher tells all the class they must not touch the sharp knife he keeps on his desk. John uses this knife to sharpen his pencil and cuts himself. Would he have cut himself if the teacher hadn't forbidden him to use this knife?

Presented with this situation, almost all the six-year-olds revealed a belief that the cut was automatic retribution for wrongdoing, whereas older children saw it as an accidental event unrelated to the rights and wrongs of John's action.

For the young child, then, what is right is what is not punished and does little damage. She has no real morality as we know it. In middle childhood she begins to define right and wrong in a different way, relying on conventional rules (you shouldn't lie, steal, cheat, break promises, etc.), but still accepting those rules as absolute and sacred. By the time she is an adolescent, she begins to understand that rules do not 'just exist' but are agreed upon by a group of people so that their group or society can function effectively; she also understands that rules can be questioned or changed, and that there are even occasions when rules can be broken if the ultimate aim is good. For example, if a man's wife is very ill but he does not have the money to pay the chemist the exorbitant amount he is asking for a drug which would cure her, the adolescent would see that there could be a case for the man attempting to steal it. An eight-year-old would equate the morality of this situation with law; a teenager observes that they are not necessarily the same thing.[12]

Psychological research on the child's concepts does not supply parents with any easy answers on how to put across notions of right and wrong; it does, however, make clear that there is often going to be a wide gulf between a child's view of a moral situation and the view of the adult. The young child cannot, for example, be expected to make much sense of her parents' reactions to her misdeeds, since they will almost always base their judgements on whether she *meant* to cause harm, and she is not yet able to think in terms of intent. Nor can she be expected to make allowances for others very easily; if she is pushed over at playgroup she is not likely to wonder whether this was an accident or not before she hits back. When she is older, at eight or nine, she may not understand things like her parent's white lie; even if the parent lied to spare hurt or embarrassment to others, she will be puzzled and perhaps angry. As an adolescent, she may be close to our way of thinking about right and wrong in many respects, but her need to question *every* rule will be infuriating unless understood in terms of her developing sense of morality. Throughout the years they are bringing up children, a knowledge of how these particular concepts develop will be of value to parents.

The child's concept of feelings

In conversation with children we often use words that describe emotions – happy, sad, jealous, angry. We use them particularly when we are trying to help the child cope with stressful situations by understanding her own feelings and those of others. But we may well wonder what in fact she makes of these 'feeling' words, and whether again her concepts are the same as ours. Research suggests that they are not, and that, like ideas of right and wrong, they develop only slowly in childhood from an initial focus on externals to some sort of grasp of internal factors and mental states. A group of Dutch psychologists[13] asked children aged six, eleven and fifteen questions about their emotions: 'How do you know if you're happy? What makes you angry? What makes you notice it? Do you feel anything inside?' Answers were classified as referring to a situation ('I'm happy 'cos it's my birthday'), a bodily reaction ('I get a headache when I'm scared'), an action ('When I'm angry I bang the table or something') and a mental state ('When I'm happy, I think everything is fine'). While children of all ages gave bodily and action definitions of emotion with equal frequency, the situational answers decreased markedly with age while the mental state answers went up. The youngest children saw feelings as made up of two components: a situation (such as a party, or a bad dream, or a quarrel) and a bodily reaction (crying, laughing and so on). They identified their own and others' feelings by using such 'visible' clues. The older children, in contrast, realized that one can smile and still be sad; they differentiated between inner states and outer appearances.

The child's concept of friendship

As with concepts of morality and emotion, the development of ideas about friendship illustrates the shift in the child's thinking from dependence on external perceptual cues to a capacity for abstract ideas, from egocentricism to an appreciation of other points of view.[14] For the young child friendship is a one-way process: a friend is a friend 'because I like her', or 'because I want her to be'. If asked to describe her friend, she will tell you what the friend looks like, or what the friend does ('She plays cars with me') but not what the friend is *like*. At this stage too anyone whom she happens to be playing with is seen as a friend, however slight the acquaintance or momentary the interaction. To make a friend, one just has to 'move in next door', or 'go and play with her'. After about the age of five, the child begins to ask a little more of friendship; a friend is now someone who does things that you like or makes you feel good. But there is as yet no notion that friendship means giving as well as taking. Not until children are nine do most mention the aspect of sharing, co-operation, helping one another, and then it will be in concrete terms: 'Well she's my friend 'cos in a fight I stick up for her and she sticks up for me', or 'We both like reading'. When she becomes able to deal in abstractions, at adolescence, she will approximate the adult concept of friendship as a relationship which is not made overnight, which involves psychological compatibility ('We're both quiet') and mutual support ('If I ever need help I know I can go to her and she can come to me').

The child's concept of time

One of the problems faced by all parents at some point is how to explain something to a child who has very limited concepts of time. She wants to know when it will be her birthday, when her friend is going to visit, when Christmas will come. She wants to explain to you something that she experienced in the past. She is told she is going to have a new brother or sister, yet nothing seems to happen for so long. Adults use words like tomorrow, last year, next week, and they mean little to her. To help with this difficulty, parents need to know what to expect: that at five many children will still be struggling with 'today', 'tomorrow' and 'yesterday', that 'next week' and 'last week' might be understood a year later, and words like 'in a fortnight', 'next year', 'last year' not until the child is eight or so.

In terms of factual knowledge, the first piece of time information the child masters is her own age (at around three); when she is five she may know what time is her bedtime and is beginning to have some idea of the days of the week; at six she might know the time she gets up; from seven on she will learn how to tell the time, what month it is, and finally what day of the month and what year. Not until she is at least eight can we expect to communicate with her about past and future events in the way we would with an adult. Until then, the child needs aids (like charts and calendars, or talk of the number of 'sleeps' until a longed-for event) to mark the passage of time. Until then, too, the parent should remember that the child has no easy way of knowing how long something might last, nor – since concepts of space and distance also take time to develop – that she knows where people are when they are not with her. Because *we* can differentiate between being away from the child for one night or ten, between being in the next town or the next county, we should not assume that the child can too. Again, parents may need to explain the things that to them need no explanation.

The child's concept of illness

Similar considerations apply when we are talking with children about illness – their own, or that of people they know. Studies have shown that they have some startling misapprehensions about the reasons people become ill. For example, in interviews with children hospitalized for heart disease and diabetes, *ninety per cent* answered the question 'Why do children get sick?' with the response 'Because they are bad'.[15] Some of these children – like the little boy at the beginning of this chapter – felt that being in hospital was a sign of rejection, or a punishment; many of them believed they were ill because they had been disobedient. Again, in another study[16] two-thirds of children aged four to sixteen (both healthy and hospitalized) blamed themselves to some extent for an illness and said that illness followed doing something you shouldn't or not doing something you should.

The reasons for this kind of thinking are not hard to find. When we talk about illness with children, it is often in terms of 'You must do your coat up or you'll catch cold', 'If you don't eat properly you'll get sick'. The child simply extrapolates from these kinds of statement: 'I'm sick *because* I didn't drink my orange juice'. She may use some extraordinary reasoning to explain how this could come about: this is one eight-year-old answering the question 'How do people get colds?' 'You're outside without a hat on and start sneezing. Your head would get cold – the cold would touch it – and then it would go all over your body.'

The question about colds was posed in one study[17] to children of various ages, between four and eleven. Several stages in the development of their understanding of illness were described. First, the youngest children (the four-year-olds) gave pre-logical answers based on the idea of magical contagion. They believed you catch diseases from people or objects ('trees . . . the sun') or 'from God . . . God does it in the sky'. You catch them simply by being near the person or object and *how* you catch them is 'just by magic'.

Older children (aged seven) added to the contagion idea that you must *touch* the source of the germs and not just be nearby. This was the age group, too, which focused particularly on illness partly resulting from engaging in a harmful action – like going out without a hat. Later in this period came the idea of germs getting *inside* the body through breathing and swallowing, but with some odd concepts about what germs actually did when they go inside: 'When you get a cold . . . bacteria get in by breathing . . . then the lungs get too soft and it goes to the nose.'

From ten to eleven on, as the child becomes increasingly able to think in abstract terms, she begins to give physiological explanations of illness: 'Other people have the virus and it gets into your bloodstream.' She will understand that illness involves not only external germs, but the body's ability to resist them. Last of all comes a grasp of the way mind and body interact: a heart attack might, for example, happen because 'You worry too much, the tension can affect your heart.'

The development of illness concepts is probably not quite so orderly and neat as this model suggests; we have only to look at attitudes to AIDS victims to see how easy it is to return to 'magical' ideas (that just being near a source of contagion is dangerous, for example) when our emotions are involved. On the whole, however, the stages outlined are a good guide to the kind of thoughts a child might have when she encounters illness, and to the kinds of misunderstanding the parent might need to tackle. They highlight the need, when a child is ill, to ask her *why* she thinks this has happened, to stress that she should not blame herself, and to give her as much information as possible.

The child's concept of death

A last area where we need to understand the special thinking of children is in their concepts of death and of dying, which though encountered much less than illness is still something most children do at some time have to confront – whether it is the death of a pet, or of an elderly neighbour, or of a person they love. As well as being hard for all of us to deal with emotionally, death is for children a particularly hard *idea* to grasp conceptually. Again, they have many misconceptions which can sometimes bring them into difficulties.[18] A mature understanding involves seeing death as a natural process which happens to all living things and is not reversible. This is unlikely to appear until the child is somewhere between the age of eight and eleven. Before this age the child may not understand that something dead cannot come to life again; she may think that dead people or animals still need food and looking after; it takes her many years to realize that death is inevitable and will happen one day to all those she cares for. When she does begin to have even an inkling of this, she may go through a period of great anxiety about the safety of loved ones.

Actual reactions to death vary a great deal in children; they have been most investigated with respect to family bereavement. Here it is found that children under five may not display grief, particularly if adults take care to assure them they will not be abandoned and will still have someone to look after them. After this age they become much more questioning and seek to understand what has happened and why, although they may not, until they are over nine, show the same emotional reactions of mourning that adults go through.[6]

Whatever the child's reaction, it is important that adults accept it and not accuse her of being uncaring if she does not show an adult type of grief. It is important too that they answer all her questions as fully and truthfully as they can, that they avoid euphemisms (like 'gone to sleep') which might add to the child's misconceptions and anxieties, and that they try to be aware of the fears about her own security, and about what might happen to others she loves, which the experience of a death may well awaken in her. Such an experience is surprisingly often found to lie behind other apparently unrelated worries or problem behaviour a child may show; in the next chapter we will be looking at some children for whom this was particularly true.

References

1 C. Zahn-Wraxler, M. Radke-Yarrow and R. King, 'Child rearing and children's prosocial initiations towards victims of distress', *Child Dev.*, 50 (1979), 319–30.
2 J. Dunn and C. Kendrick, *Siblings: Love, Envy and Understanding*, Cambridge, Massachusetts, Harvard University Press, 1982.
3 S. K. Thompson, 'Gender labels and early sex-role development', *Child Dev.*, 46 (1975), 339–47.
4 J. H. Flavell, *The Developmental Psychology of Jean Piaget*, Princeton, New Jersey, Van Nostrand, 1963.
5 M. Hughes and M. Donaldson, 'The use of hiding games for studying the co-ordination of viewpoints, *Ed. Review*, 31 (1979), 133–40.
6 S. Wolff, *Children under Stress*, 2nd edn., Harmondsworth, Penguin Books, 1973.
7 A. Aggernaes and R. Haugsted, 'Experienced reality in three- to six-year-old children: a study of direct reality testing'. *J. Child Psychol. Psychiatry*, 17 (1976), 323–35.
8 M. Donaldson, *Children's Minds*, Glasgow, Fontana/Collins, 1978.
9 J. Bruner, *The Relevance of Education*, New York, Norton, 1971.
10 J. Piaget and B. Inhelder, *The Psychology of the Child*, London, Routledge and Kegan Paul, 1969.
11 J. Piaget, *The Moral Judgement of the Child*, London, Kegan Paul, 1932.
12 L. Kohlberg, 'The development of children's orientation towards a moral order. I: Sequence in the development of human thought', *Vita Humana*, 6 (1963), 11–33.
13 P. L. Harris, T. Olthof and M. M. Terwogt, 'Children's knowledge of emotion', *J. Child Psychol. Psychiatry*, 22 (1981), 247–61.

14 R. Selman and D. Jaquette, 'The development of interpersonal awareness —
working draft of manual, Harvard-Judge Baker Social Reasoning project',
quoted in Z. Rubin *Children's Friendships*, London, Open Books/Fontana, 1980.
15 B. Beverley, 'The effects of illness upon emotional development', *J. Paediatrics*, 8
(1936), 533.
16 E. Gellert, 'Children's beliefs about bodily illness', paper presented at the 1965
meeting of the American Psychological Association, quoted in E. C. Perrin and
P. S. Gerrity, 'There's a demon in your belly', *Paediatrics*, 67 (1981), 841–9.
17 R. Bibace and M. E. Walsh, 'The Development of children's concepts of illness',
Paediatrics, 66 (1980), 912–17.
18 R. Kastenbaum and R. Aisenberg, *Psychology of Death*, New York, Springer
Publishing, 1972.

11 Fears

Sarah, aged four, and normally a confident and sociable little girl, had become most reluctant to leave her mother to go to nursery school or visit friends. Even at birthday parties she insisted that her mother stay with her. Just before all this began, she had woken in the night with a bad dream. In her dream, she said, everyone in the family got sick and somebody died. At first she would not tell her mother who, but eventually she managed to say 'It was you'. Looking further back, her mother remembered how there had been a reference in a family service at church to the tragic illness and death of a young man from the congregation. The connection was plain. Sarah had become genuinely frightened of some harm coming to her mother and wanted to stay close by her to make sure she would be safe.

Another very small boy was terrified of the bath; he cried and fought if his parents tried to bathe him. Ultimately it emerged that he was frightened in case he went down the plughole. His reasoning was simple: if the water can disappear down that dark hole, why can't I?.[1]

With their limited understanding and their different ways of thinking, children do easily become afraid. Sometimes it takes a major leap of the imagination to guess at the source of their sudden terrors. Sometimes parents need not only understanding, but also techniques that will help them calm a fearful child and teach him how to cope with anxiety. In this chapter we will consider how the theories and the practice of psychologists treating severe fears and phobias can help ordinary parents deal with the more commonplace, but still bothersome, fears that their children are likely to show.

Common fears

Fears are particularly common in the pre-school years. Three is the peak age:

in one survey over half of three-year-olds were said by their parents to have at least one specific fear.[2] By the age of six this figure fell to one in ten. The things children fear change with their age; infants are afraid of sudden noises, of falling, of strange objects and people. But these fears reach a peak before the age of two, then decline, to be replaced by a characteristic group of fears to do with animals and insects (peaking at three years and sometimes persisting from this age right into adulthood), the dark (peaking at four) and imaginary creatures (peaking at five).[3] These preschool years are the time for fear of ghosts, monsters and witches; this is the period of fearsome patterns in the wallpaper when the lights are out, of tigers chasing you upstairs and beasts lurking behind corners – what adults label dismissively as 'imaginary fears'.

In the school years the fears of imaginary creatures decrease and fears become more realistic, having to do with possible physical harm or danger. Fears about school (teachers, coping with work, speaking in public) become more common, particularly between the ages nine to twelve.[4] Adolescents also fear being hurt, or ill, or incapacitated, but they begin now to show some more adult anxieties – such as fear of open or closed spaces, or social occasions – which hardly appear at all in early or middle childhood. Very conscious of their role in the group, they fear being ridiculed, or being the subject of gossip, and their fears may become so great that they are unable to take part in normal teenage social activities.

The most widespread fear of all, running right through all the age groups, is the fear of losing loved ones, of being alone or abandoned. This is a very secret fear, and one which parents are often unaware of. In the clinical experience of those who work with troubled children, it comes up again and again – whether it be the fear (like Sarah's) of the parent dying, or the fear (like that of some adopted children) of being given or sent away if they are not good, or the anxiety of the older child who sees any parental quarrel as a sign that one parent might depart.[7] If the child has been rendered vulnerable by past unhappy separations, such fears are particularly likely:

> Alan was nine but still reacted badly when his parents planned to go out for the evening: he would sulk, or cry, or even become angry with them to an extent that they had almost given up having a social life together. He had been like this on and off all his life but had become worse lately ever since his mother had to spend a few days in hospital, and since he had heard his older brothers talk about the death in a car-crash of one of their friends. He had become preoccupied with the idea of car accidents and always commented on damaged cars he saw on the road. He had as a baby, his mother recalled, had several short hospital admissions in the days when parents were not allowed to stay in with their young children. Although long forgotten, these separations had left an uncertainty in Alan's mind which recent events seemed to have reactivated.

Theories of fear

There is little doubt that some children are temperamentally more prone to fearfulness than others, and that these temperamental variations have a biological basis and can to some extent be inherited.[5] If a parent is a worrier, there is an increased chance his or her children will be too – although a good part of this may be due to the child's learning, by direct observation and imitation of his mother or father, to react to new situations with anxiety.

Some psychologists view all fears and worries as learned behaviour. Fears can be acquired, it is thought, either by imitation or as a result of the association of a previously neutral with a noxious event – like the little boy in a classic case described in the 1920s in whom a fear of a white rat was artificially created by pairing its presence with an unpleasant, loud noise.[6] A fear of bees after being stung, of the dentist after a painful filling, of having one's hair washed after getting soap in the eyes would all be examples of this kind of learned fear. So would be some overgeneralized fears, such as that of the child who became terrified of *all* balloons after a gas balloon was used by the anaesthetist when he was in hospital for a minor operation.[7]

Other theorists, noting that many fears seem quite unrelated to unpleasant experiences, and wondering why, for example, so many adults are afraid of quite harmless spiders, and why a child who had never before seen either would be much more likely to be frightened of a snake than a fish, consider that there are some *instinctive* fear arousers. In particular, in an important book on the subject,[7] Dr John Bowlby has developed a theory that we are all prone to fear the things which long ago in man's earliest days were associated with danger. To be afraid of, and to avoid, sudden noises, or rapid approach by a person/animal, or reptiles and insects, or darkness, would increase man's chances of survival: in evolutionary terms such fears were useful. The absence or loss of a protective figure would always signal increased danger to the young, the weak and the helpless; this above all came to be a source of anxiety. If all this is true, Bowlby points out, then the fears which we call childish and irrational are in fact part of our oldest inheritance and once helped man to survive in what was then a much more hostile environment.

Some fears seem to be connected with unusual events – discrepancies from our expectations. An eight-month-old baby may be frightened the first time she sees her mother in sunglasses. Many children are terrified for a while of masks. The four-year-olds in the Newsons' Nottingham Study[1] were particularly afraid of what they called 'the abnormal state of normal objects', such as a burnt-down house or broken things. Slight variations from the norm can cause us fear; at other times the same variations might make us feel only surprise or even make us laugh, as the older child will laugh at a mask or a parent making funny faces. Such deviations – the familiar in unfamiliar guise – arouse tension on a continuum from mild surprise to genuine fear. Laughter is one way of releasing this tension. The older child laughs when the jack-in-the-box pops out; the infant may cry loudly with fright.

Another theory, which we met in chapter 8, links children's fears, like their dreams and nightmares, with their own jealous and angry thoughts: the monster lying in wait in the dark is both the projection of the monster inside the child, and the fantasy figure who will punish him for his wickedness.[7] It is an attractive theory, particularly for those imaginary fears of the pre-school years, although it is perhaps equally possible to explain these in terms of the as yet unclear boundary which the child draws between what is real and what is not. He may simply not *know* that the ogres and giants and fierce animals he hears of in stories and sees on television cannot really be hiding behind the curtains.

Fears and phobias

Phobias are not the same as fears – though many of the fears of the two- and three-year-old might be called phobias if shown by an adult. What distinguishes a phobia from a fear is the intensity of dread evoked by a particular object or situation, in relation to the degree of dread it evokes in others. If most young children fear the dark, we could not call their fear a phobia. The other distinguishing feature of a true phobia is that it begins to take over a child or adult's life, making it difficult for them to act normally. A great many children are afraid of large dogs, but this is not a problem unless they avoid going anywhere they might even see a dog, can't enjoy being out in case they do or start to be afraid of other kinds of furry animals, furry materials, even fur coats, as well – like Colleen in this example:[8]

> Colleen was eleven and was almost housebound as a result of her five-year fear of dogs. On Sunday evenings she would begin to worry in case she might meet a dog on her way to the bus stop next morning; at school she was constantly on edge about the journey home, and she could not concentrate. She seldom went out to play with friends and would never play outdoors. Her parents could not recall any incident which started off the fear, although an aunt was reported to be afraid of cats and dogs, and Colleen's mother was agoraphobic and abnormally compulsive about her household chores.

Phobias may need professional treatment; it is possible, however, for parents to prevent many ordinary everyday fears from escalating into phobias if they are able to step in quickly and help the child master his anxiety before it masters him.

Understanding fears and reflecting feelings

The first step in helping a child to overcome a fear is for the parent to acknowledge and respect the reality of the child's feelings. It is common for children to be teased and belittled for their fears; it is common for attempts to be made to force them very abruptly into feared situations – as with the small boy whose father throws him crying into the swimming pool so that he will lose his fear of water. A more useful approach is to begin with the kind of reflective listening described in chapter 9 ('I know it's very hard for you to think of getting into the water') coupled with a message which emphasizes the child's own ability to cope and your intention of helping him to do so ('. . . but I'm sure you're going to manage it because you always do manage things; I know some special things you can try which will help'). Sometimes the acknowledgement of feelings will also mean trying to understand the source of a fear, so that an acceptance of its hidden message can also be communicated ('I know you don't want to go to the party by yourself; I wonder if that has anything to do with the worry you sometimes have about something happening to me'). The parents will want to consider whether the fear is simply a learned association with an unpleasant or painful event, whether it could be due (like the little boy and the bathplug) to a cognitive misunderstanding they can set right, or whether it is a surface sign of some other, deeper anxiety. An explanation of how fears can arise may be helpful, particularly to older children and teenagers, as it was with Maureen:

> Maureen, aged sixteen, had collapsed in the street with a tummy bug whilst on holiday with her family in Spain. Since then, she had become very anxious about going out in her home town, particularly about using public transport, and was spending more and more of her time in the house. If she tried to go out, she expressed panic and began to feel physically ill. She could not understand why she felt this way. Her mother explained to her that the experience on holiday had been so unpleasant that it taught her body to feel very scared when she was out in public. She also explained to Maureen that part of the feeling of being scared is our body's preparation to take emergency action to combat danger – the 'fight-or-flight' response which includes rapid breathing, accelerated heartbeat and a temporary halt in the activity of the digestive system. This might be experienced in many ways: a pounding heart, sweaty palms, a dry mouth, weak knees, knots or butterflies in the stomach, a lump in the throat, nausea. Maureen had perhaps felt some of these things when she was out and had interpreted them as a sign that she was going to be ill in public again, rather than as just her body's natural physiological response. A circular situation had been established, where her fear made her feel bad and feeling bad augmented her fear.

Teaching relaxation

After explaining the physiology of fear, Maureen's mother went on to show
her how to slow down the fight-or-flight response and stop her body from
overreacting. The techniques she taught her were a particular kind of
breathing and progressive muscle relaxation.

Familiar to most mothers and some fathers from ante-natal classes, these
relaxation techniques are well worth teaching to any child over the age of
four or five, and particularly to the 'worriers' or to those with specific fears.
The parent should first discuss with the child how he can recognize that he is
upset or worried by noticing the physical signs described above. Then all that
is needed is to explain that breathing slowly and deeply will trick the body
out of its attempt to 'get ready to run, or get ready to fight' and will have an
immediate calming effect. The parent should demonstrate, using a hand
placed first on the upper and then on the lower part of the chest, that there
are two kinds of breathing: the shallow panicky kind which does not push the
lower chest in and out at all, and the deep calm breathing which does. The
child can practise the deeper breathing, counting 'one, two' slowly with the
parent and trying to push away the hand on his lower chest, just above the
waist.

He should be told to begin to breathe in this way as soon as he starts to feel
tense or upset and to continue until his heart stops pounding and the
butterflies in the stomach disappear.

Children can also quite easily be taught progressive relaxation, how to
tense and tighten each group of muscles in turn from the toes upwards, then
to let those muscles go floppy and loose. Lying in bed worrying about
tomorrow's PE lesson or next week's exam, they can combine slow breathing
with this kind of relaxation to good effect.

Taking control

Teaching a child relaxation techniques is one way of giving him control over
potentially stressful situations. Psychological research has demonstrated
that it is the situations which we cannot control which we find most
frightening: that the dog on a lead which he can approach at his own pace
will not trouble the child, whereas the same dog unleashed and bounding up
to him may cause panic. In an interesting experiment,[9] one-year-old
children were introduced to a novel toy – a mechanical monkey which
clapped cymbals – in one of two conditions: either the experimenter pressed
the button to start the monkey clapping, or the child did. Many of the
children (particularly the boys) were frightened by this toy, but being in
control of it much reduced their distress.

Parents then need to find ways in which the child can take charge of his fear. Finding something which he can say to himself in a frightening situation can be surprisingly helpful:[10] 'I am brave. I can manage. I am not going to be scared.' Finding something which he can *do* may be the second step:

> Diane, aged four, had been waking in the night with bad dreams for several weeks. She would come into her parents' room crying and describing the ghost which had figured in the dreams ever since her older sister had gone through a phase of telling ghost stories. Diane's parents discussed with her what she might say to the ghost, and it was decided that she would shout 'Boo!' very loudly when it appeared, since ghosts would always go away if you did that. This seemed to help, and within a few days the dreams had stopped.

Desensitization: a gradual approach to fears

In treating fears in adults and children, psychologists have found that an essential part of the treatment must be a confrontation with the feared object or situation: it is the experience of confrontation and the finding that *nothing terrible happens* which brings the cure. How the confrontation is arranged, however, needs careful thought. Throwing the child straight into the swimming pool may not be the best way to go about teaching him to like swimming. His fear of water could be handled in a different way:

> James was a mentally handicapped six-year-old who refused to join his friends in the water at their weekly swimming lesson and screamed loudly if attempts were made to get him near the pool. His teacher decided to introduce him to the idea very gradually; the first week she just gave him a bowl of water and some toys to play with at some distance from the edge of the pool. He enjoyed this, and over succeeding weeks she brought the bowl closer until he was playing very near the edge. She then joined in his play and introduced splashing games; soon he would sit on her lap at the edge of the pool while they played together. The next step was for them both to have their toes in the pool as they splashed and played with the toys and the bowl, then their feet, their legs. James began to like kicking and splashing and was soon willing to slide in briefly into a helper's arms. It took several more weeks until he would stay in the water, held by the helper, and several more until he would go in alone, but by the end of the school year he had lost all his fear and was first into the bus on swimming days.

The idea behind this way of tackling fears is to construct a hierarchy of experiences which will lead the child to confront the feared object by very small steps. Any parent who has bought a puppy to help a child overcome a terror of dogs has used the desensitization idea: the child gets accustomed to dogs by stages, starting with a manageable approximation too small to fear and learning as the puppy grows that dogs are not so frightening after all.

Many parents also use desensitization to combat fears of doctors and dentists: the child is allowed to sit for a short time in the dentist's chair, to handle all his instruments, to watch his mother having a filling, until he is ready to have one himself.

A parent whose child has a specific fear that is presenting problems to him or his family can construct, and write down, a hierarchy of experiences to approximate the feared object. The gradient of experience can be one of proximity (getting slowly closer to a real live rabbit, for example, as in the following case of Peter), or of similarity (playing first with a toy stuffed rabbit, making pictures out of fur fabric, handling mother's fur coat). Using other children or adults to provide a fearless model for the child to imitate can be helpful:

> Peter, aged nearly three, was introduced to a playroom with three other children, none of whom shared his fear of furry animals. A white rabbit in a cage was brought into the room and placed near the door. Peter did not go near it, but he watched the others when they did. At a later session the cage was moved closer to the toys, and closer again until Peter was playing happily alongside the cage. In the next session an adult held the rabbit while Peter's three friends stroked it. In subsequent weeks Peter himself touched the rabbit, helped the adult put it back in its cage, held it on his own lap, stayed alone in the room with it and allowed it to nibble his fingers.[11]

In order to help the child relax as a feared object or situation comes nearer, he can be encouraged to use relaxation techniques, or he can be given something nice to do which is incompatible with tensing up – like eating crisps or a sweet:

> Billy, aged eight, was afraid of cars and would not set foot in one. The fear dated from a car accident two years before. He was treated by a psychologist who engaged him in talk first about vehicles other than cars: when Billy said anything positive about tractors, motorbikes or whatever, he was offered a small piece of chocolate. He then played with toy cars, enacting accidents and being given chocolate from time to time. This play continued until the psychologist was able to persuade Billy to sit with him for a few minutes in a stationary car. In the next session he went for a short ride in the car, and later for a longer drive to a shop where he bought some chocolate.[12]

Billy's treatment combined the relaxing effects of eating with the positive-reward value of chocolate to help him overcome a long-standing fear. Star-chart systems geared to an eventual reward can also be used to motivate the child: he can draw up a list of the steps in the hierarchy that leads up to confrontation and colour in a square or stick on a star when he has completed each step.

Even without his parents' involvement a child will often desensitize himself by playing out his fears over and over again until he has got accustomed to the frightening idea. The role of the parent then is to provide the right toys and a setting where he has time, space and companions to play this sort of pretend game. After he has been in hospital, for example, he needs to play at doctors and nurses, and to be supplied with essential props like bits of sheet for bandages and coloured water for nasty medicine.

The secure base

If, as Dr Bowlby suggests, a lack of confidence in the availability of his attachment figures is a prime source of anxiety in the child, one aspect of handling fears must be taking care to foster that confidence early on and to maintain it as the child grows. The child needs to be sure that the parent – or substitute attachment figure – will be around when needed. How he acquires, or fails to acquire, this certainty is a complex process. It begins in infancy; important research by Mary Ainsworth and her colleagues[12] suggests that it starts with something called 'responsive' parenting: attending reliably and sensitively to the baby's signals. It continues in the way in which necessary separations and absences are handled in the pre-school years: who takes care of the child when his parents aren't there, how familiar and reliable is the substitute caretaker, how well the child is prepared for separations.[13] It would be undermined in the all too common situation where the parent makes a habit of slipping off without warning the child – as soon as he is playing happily at a friend's house or at playgroup, for example. The parent who does slip off may be avoiding an immediate tearful scene, but he or she is creating for the future an anxious child who is never quite sure when he might look round and find himself frighteningly alone. Pushing a child into a premature independence may also be counterproductive: there is now a good deal of research which shows that it is the toddler with a very secure attachment base who two or three years later is *less* likely to be clingy and dependent than his peers.[14] Tolerating early dependency, thinking carefully about separations, always letting the young child know when and where you are going, and avoiding (even in the heat of the moment) any threat, at any age, to leave or abandon or send the child away ('I've had enough of you', 'You'll be the death of me') – all these are important in producing a confident and relatively fearless child.

School fears

Many parents will at some point face a situation where the child does not want to go to school and seems genuinely afraid, claims illness, has an upset tummy or a sudden headache. Some parents will face a more acute version, sometimes called school phobia or school refusal, where they cannot get the child to school at all: where he cries and hides, or tries to run away, or even vomits at the school gates.

It is because fears about going to school are so common that it is important for parents to know how to handle them. Terence Moore, studying a group of children's development over a period of several years, found that as many as eighty per cent experienced difficulties in adjustment in the infant school and were at some time very reluctant to attend.[15] Their reluctance peaked at the age of six, then declined, with another peak at eight years on the change to junior school. Since Moore's study, the more widespread availability of nursery schools and playgroups may have pushed backwards in time the anxieties that so many children in the sixties showed on starting school at five; a more recent study of over six thousand Buckinghamshire children[16] found that dislike of school varied little with age over the five-to-fifteen year range. It was more common in boys, particularly boys who were not doing well academically; it was associated with signs of anxiety at home and a great many possibly psychosomatic headaches and stomach pains.

A reluctance to go to school may stem from specific problems within the school itself (relationships with teachers, trouble with peers, dislike of school dinners, of using school toilets, trouble with work, with PE lessons), *or* from a reluctance to leave home. In the latter case what the child fears is not so much events at school, but being away from his family: he may be an overdependent child with very protective parents, or he may have a history of stressful separations in early childhood, or there may have been recent loss or illness in the family which makes him feel a need to stay close to those he loves.[17]

Discovering whether the child is afraid of going to school, of leaving home, or of a mixture of both may mean looking at his past history, at events in the family, and at his reactions to other separations – asking, for example, whether he has a regular stomach-ache on Tuesday mornings before a history lesson, or whether he is generally reluctant to go out at all, even for non-school social events. If the anxiety seems to be related to happenings in school, these should be discussed with the headteacher and the staff who will often be able to help. If the real anxiety is not school at all, the parent can try through reflective listening to share this awareness with the child and to open up some communication on issues of dependency, of loss and of separation.

In either event it is important at all cost to make sure, when the problem starts, that the child does go on attending school, however difficult this may be for him or for you. Staying away magnifies the fears and perpetuates whatever symptoms – physical or behavioural – that the child is using (not necessarily consciously) in order to remain at home. Communicate, teach relaxation, talk to the school – but *get him there*, even if this means hysterics or worse. If you are not sure whether he really has a stomach-ache or not, explain this to the teacher and ask her to keep an eye on him, letting you know if he seems really ill – but take him to school. If you feel unable to cope with his panic, ask someone else (the other parent, or a neighbour, or an education welfare officer) if they will escort him for a few days. Establish a positive reward system as well: at first with a small reward for each day of going to school without fuss, and later with a star chart covering several days or a week at a time.

The child who has stopped going to school altogether presents greater difficulties: this is why it is best to be very firm about going to school at the first sign of fears. If the child has been out of school for some time, desensitization combined with a powerful reward system may get him back:[17] he should construct a hierarchy beginning with walking past the school, or sitting in a car outside practising relaxation, then sitting for five minutes perhaps in the school secretary's office or another neutral spot with a friendly teacher with whom he has a good relationship, attending a lesson given by that teacher, and so on up to a full day's attendance. His friends can be told that he has been ill and has to come back to school slowly. But such techniques need very careful planning and co-operation from the school and may succeed only if the family has outside support; for these reasons it may be necessary to seek professional help.

References

1 J. Newson and E. Newson, *Four Years Old in an Urban Community*, London, Allen and Unwin, 1968.
2 J. W. MacFarlane, L. Allen and M. R. Honzik, *A Developmental Study of the Behaviour Problems of Normal Children*, California, University of California Press, 1954.
3 A. T. Jersild and F. B. Holmes, *Children's Fears*, New York, Teachers' College, 1935.
4 L. Hersov, 'Emotional disorders', in M. Rutter and L. Hersov (eds.), *Child and Adolescent Psychiatry: Modern Approaches*, 2nd edn., Oxford, Blackwell Scientific Publications, 1985.
5 A. Thomas, S. Chess and H. G. Birch, *Temperament and Behaviour Disorders in Children*, New York Universities Press, 1968.
6 J. B. Watson and R. Raynes, 'Conditioned emotional reactions', *J. Exp. Psychol.*, 3 (1920), 1–14.
7 J. Bowlby, *Attachment and Loss*, vol 2. *Separation: Anxiety and Anger*, London, Hogarth Press, 1973.
8 U. Screenivasan, S. Manocha and V. K. Jain, 'Treatment of severe dog phobia in childhood by flooding: a case report', *J. Child Psychol. Psychiatry*, 20 (1979), 255–60.
9 M. R. Gunnar-Vongnechten, 'Changing a frightening toy into a pleasant toy by allowing the infant to control its actions', *Develop. Psychol.*, 14 (1978), 157–62.
10 A. M. Graziano and K. C. Mooney, 'Family self-control instruction for children's night-time fear reduction', *J. Consult. Clin. Psychol.*, 48 (1980), 206–13.

11 M. C. Jones, 'A laboratory study of fear: the case of Peter', *Pedagogical Seminary*, 31 (1924), 308–15.

12 M. C. Blehar, A. F. Lieberman and M. D. S. Ainsworth, 'Early face-to-face interaction and its relation to later infant–mother attachment', *Child Dev.*, 48 (1977), 182–94.

13 J. Robertson and J. Robertson, 'Young children in brief separations: a fresh look', *Psychoanal. Study Child*, 26 (1971), 262–315.

14 L. A. Sroufe, M. E. Fox and V. R. Pancake, 'Attachment and dependency in developmental perspective', *Child Dev.*, 54 (1983), 1615–27.

15 T. Moore, 'Difficulties of the ordinary child in adjusting to primary school', *J. Child Psychol. Psychiatry*, 7 (1966), 17–38.

16 S. Mitchell and M. Shepherd, 'Reluctance to go to school' in L. Hersov and I. Berg (eds.), *Out of School – Modern Perspectives in School Refusal and Truancy*, Chichester, Wiley, 1980.

17 L. Hersov, 'School refusal', in M. Rutter and L. Hersov (eds.), *Child and Adolescent Psychiatry: Modern Approaches*, 2nd edn., Oxford, Blackwell Scientific Publications, 1985.

12 Habits

Children's habits – thumb or finger sucking, nailbiting, having to have a particular 'cuddly' with them everywhere they go – often cause problems between them and their parents. Many parents find themselves particularly irritated by these habits, yet feel uncertain about whether it is right to try to break the habit and vaguely guilty if they do keep telling the child to stop. Very often the result of this uncertainty is that the habit (and the child) become the focus of some irritable, inconsistent, on-and-off nagging: the child doesn't change what she is doing but is uncomfortably aware that she is the object of disapproval. Parents do not know what to think; they worry in case the child's habit is a sign of tension or unmet emotional needs; they have heard that it is wise to ignore troublesome habits but ignoring has not helped so far. Yet there is a good deal of research on these habits; much of it addresses the same questions that parents ask themselves, so that the findings are indeed useful in helping us know what – if anything – we should do about a persistent hair twiddler, finger sucker, fluff-picker, blanket-clutcher or whatever.

Cuddlies

Many families are intimately acquainted with cuddlies – those (usually) soft objects, ranging from bits of blanket to a toy alligator, to a powder puff, to Dad's old silk tie, to which young children often show a real and long-lasting emotional attachment. If a child does have a cuddly (and the numbers who do can be anything from fifteen to sixty per cent, with a peak incidence at two to three years),[1] it will for quite some time be an important part of family life, almost like another member of the family, given a name by the child (very individual names, like 'teddy teesh' for a piece of a teddy bear's silky shirt, or 'ging' for a rag made of checked gingham), a source of comfort in times of stress, essential at bedtime, deeply missed if lost or left behind.

All theories about cuddlies share an assumption that the cuddly helps the child bridge the gap left by the parent's temporary absence: that in some way it 'stands for' the complex of good feelings a child has experienced in the past when close to her mother. There may, it is thought, be an innate tendency in all primates to seek out and cling to soft objects of any kind;[2] alternatively the cuddly may be a learned object of attachment – learned by association or generalization, because it feels a little bit like the touch of the mother's skin, or the feel of her dress while the baby was feeding, because it has the human smell she associates with being held and fed, or because the infant fingered the object itself at times when she was feeling particularly comfortable and content. Psychoanalytic theories, notably those of Dr D. W. Winnicott,[3] see the cuddly as something of much greater importance than just a byproduct of conditioning; recognizing its meaning to the child as something that is uniquely *hers*, that she chooses and names and needs, Winnicott stresses that cuddlies are a sign of the child's movement away from total dependence on and togetherness with the mother, towards a point where she can see herself as a wholly separate person. The cuddly is part of a gradual weaning process, a half-way house; it is also the child's first real possession, her first statement about her own identity, her first creation.

All these theories make cuddlies sound eminently useful and emotionally healthy, and indeed research supports this idea. On the whole, children who have had cuddlies in their pre-school years are found to be slightly *better* adjusted than those who have not;[4,5] this relationship holds even with social class held constant (a necessary control since cuddlies are more common in middle-class children than in under privileged families, as is 'adjustment'). In one study, for example, John and Elizabeth Newson[5] followed up a large group of four-year-olds over a seven-year period. Cuddly-users were identified by asking their parents if the child insisted something accompany him or her to bed each night. Those who were cuddly-users at four were at eleven less timid, less likely to show signs of nervous tension (tics, headaches, nightmares) and less likely to be 'worriers' than those who had not had a cuddly. Far from being a sign of insecurity or psychological difficulties, the blanket or ribbon or toy panda was found to be associated with later stability and sociability.

There is no real need, then, for the parent to think that he or she ought to wean a child away from a cuddly, and certainly no justification for abruptly throwing that old bit of rag away because it has become a nuisance. Most children, however, do cope quite easily with the idea that their cuddly stays at home (or even stays in the bedroom) and does not go with them to friends' houses, or to playgroup – though it will come with them on holidays or overnight visits. This kind of rule does help avoid the practical problems posed by a child who can do nothing and go nowhere without a cuddly. It is also a reasonable rule: after all, there are times when she can have you, the parent, and times when she can't, and so it is with her comfort object. Like all rules, this one must be consistently applied: the child will be confused if she is one day allowed the cuddly in the car and the next day not, according to the parent's convenience. If, despite such consistency, the child seems quite unable to cope without her cuddly while she is out, it is likely that too much is being asked of her: she is too tired, or facing too long a separation from you, or too many new people or experiences all at once. In this case she would be better out of the situation altogether, rather than miserably clutching her rag in a corner.

Sucking habits – thumbs, fingers and dummies

Sucking is to the young child pleasurable in itself, and because it is rhythmic and repetitive it is also soothing and helps her relax and sleep. Most babies have some kind of sucking habit, whether it is dummy or fingers or thumb that they use. There is evidence of some kind of biological variation in the enjoyment of sucking – some babies having very early, strong sucking habits, others not wanting to suck for milk and having to be spoon-fed from the beginning.[5] There is evidence, too, that a tendency to thumb-sucking can run in families, so that the influence of heredity might help to explain why some children acquire the habit and some don't.[6]

Most parents actively encourage one or other sucking habit when their children are babies. It is later, however, that the problems come. Many children do give up the habit spontaneously, but not all. One in three four-year-olds still suck thumb, dummy or fingers;[5] by the age of ten a third of these will still be sucking their thumb.[7] The parents of these children are often ashamed to see the child acting in a way they feel is babyish; they may come actively to dislike the sight of their large five-year-old sitting with a glazed and vacant expression sucking her thumb and twiddling her hair, or stroking her rag or a bit of fluff against her lips or nose.

Cuddlies and thumb- or finger-sucking are often closely related: indeed one of the reasons why children get attached to their cuddlies is because the cuddly (like the silky edge of a cot blanket) is clutched in the hand that is sucked – it literally 'gets caught up in the sucking habit'.[1] Thumbs, too, can come to stand for the absent mother, as with the two-year-old who called her thumb her 'mummy's coming'. Nevertheless, persistent sucking habits do not seem to be quite as emotionally healthy as having a cuddly *per se*. The evidence on this point is somewhat inconsistent: there is certainly no overrepresentation of thumb- and finger-suckers in children referred to psychiatrists,[7,8] or in children with reported 'psychological problems',[9] nor do thumb-suckers seem to be more anxious or tense than non-suckers.[10] But in the Newsons' study of cuddlies and sucking habits, the thirty per cent of four-year-olds who were still regularly sucking dummy or fingers were found to be somewhat more awkward and moody on follow-up at the ages of eleven and sixteen than non-suckers. (This study also found, interestingly, that this group were *not* more likely to have taken up smoking at the age of sixteen: evidence against any assumption we might make that there is a generalized and life-long tendency to 'oral habits' of all kinds).

Persistent sucking habits, then, are not, as far as we can see, associated with current emotional insecurity, as is sometimes suggested, but nor are they associated with positive long-term emotional adjustment either. There is no need for the parents of a thumb-sucker to feel she is somehow lacking in comfort elsewhere, or that she may be tense and worried. On the other hand, there are no particular psychological reasons *against* their helping her to give up the habit. Since there are strong dental reasons for giving up (evidence that persistent sucking will make the teeth grow out of alignment),[11] it seems that this is something parents should indeed ask of the child. Helping her stop sucking will also prevent her from being teased by friends and may improve parent–child relationships if they are strained as a result of the parent's irritation and nagging.

Dummies are easy to tackle: they can simply be kept at home, like the cuddly, and later confined to bedtimes; then later still thrown away altogether. Thumbs are much more difficult; they go everywhere. A confirmed thumb-sucker will not give up easily just because she is told about sticking out teeth or told off whenever the thumb goes in. Like an adult giving up cigarettes, she needs to use a good deal of will-power to kick the habit. She needs all the help she can get: the following approach is one which has worked for many children, and which parents might like to try.

- Begin if possible when the child is four or five before the second teeth arrive, and before she starts school.
- Discuss with her the reasons for giving up: teeth and looking babyish.
- Choose a time when the child is relaxed and under your eye most of the time: for older children school holidays are the best time.
- Tell the child she has a big task ahead of her, and that it will help her if she has a big reward at the end. Let her choose a fairly big 'prize': a toy she has wanted for a long time, for example. Buy it and put it in a cupboard.
- Make a star chart for about thirty days.

M	T	W	T	F	S	S	M	T	W
T	F	S	S	M	T	W	T	F	S
S	M	T	W	T	F	S	S	M	T

- Give the child something else to do with her hands at times when she usually sucks (watching television, in the car): worry-beads, or Rubik's cube, or any other fiddly executive toy. At bedtime suggest she holds on to a cuddly toy.
- Paint her thumb or fingers regularly, several times a day, with an anti nail-biting liquid (available from chemists).
- Praise the child for each day she can colour in a square, stick on a star, or paint in the finger nail of a drawn thumb on her chart, for *not sucking* at all that day. Give her also an immediate small reward like a special chocolate.
- Let her know that you understand how hard all this is for her, and how she must be feeling. Keep reminding her of the big prize. If she does slip up, say nothing other than that she can't colour in the square for that day.
- At the end of twenty consecutive non-sucking days she gets the prize. In practice, once she has gone a few days without sucking she is unlikely to revert: she will find it 'feels funny' if she does try to suck again.

Nail-biting

Nail-biting is very common in childhood: as many as one in three children of school age bite their nails regularly.[7] More so even than thumb-sucking, it is often said to be a sign of nervous tension but, although it is true that a persistent nail-biter will frequently begin to nibble when he or she is worried or feels shy, stopping when the awkward moment has passed, there is again no clear *general* association between nail-biting and emotional adjustment.[7] As a group, nail-biters are not more neurotic or disturbed than other children. Genetic make-up seems to play a part in this habit too: in twin studies it has been found that identical twins (with identical genes) are much more alike in whether or not they bite their nails than are fraternal twins (with different genes).[12]

As with thumb-sucking, constantly saying 'Will you stop that' rarely works, but a reward system (tied in to providing an alternative that keeps the hands busy) is likely to succeed. The cure, however, will in this case rarely be permanent, and the programme may have to be repeated every six months or so. For this reason, a smaller prize than for thumb-sucking would be a good idea. If possible, the prize should be something which is linked with the reason for giving up nail-biting. For boys, this might be a penknife that needs finger-nails to pull out its many attachments; for girls it could be sparkly nail polish, a manicure set, or a ring that will look good on attractive hands. Having her mother show her how to care for her hands and paint her nails on Fridays, so that she can wear nail polish all weekend, is another good reward to use with a girl on a weekly basis, if her nails have obviously not been chewed over the week.

Other habits

The standard advice for the many other odd and individual habits (from headbanging to teeth grinding, to making funny noises) which children develop from time to time is to ignore the behaviour and avoid making any sort of fuss about it. In some cases this works, but not always: by the time the parent finds out that his or her attention doesn't seem to be acting as a reward for this particular behaviour, the habit is usually firmly entrenched. Habits can begin by accident, but the longer they go on the harder they are to get rid of. For this reason, stepping in quickly with a reward system is often the best thing to do, as in this example:

> Paula, aged five, began one winter to complain that her fingers 'felt dry', and every few minutes would put them in her mouth for a downward lick that soon made the whole area below her mouth red and sore. The habit looked most peculiar, but Paula's father remembered that he had done the same thing as a child. Ignoring did not help Paula to stop; nor did handcream. Wearing gloves in the house would help for a while, but eventually she would take them off and start to lick again. What did work, however, was a very simple promise: one chocolate mint at lunchtime if she hadn't licked all morning, and one in the evening if she hadn't licked all afternoon.

Paula's ability to control, on the promise of a reward, what looked like a purely involuntary nervous habit came as a surprise to her parents. Yet this sort of result with a reward programme is not at all uncommon. More often than not, a child can break herself of a habit *if* we help her by making the effort worthwhile.

A final group of habits which often cause problems are those, like masturbation and nose-picking, to which the best response is an explanation that they are private things, only to be done in private. Masturbation in young children is very common, especially in boys: over half the pre-school boys in one study, for example, showed some kind of masturbatory activity, and one in six girls.[13] In these enlightened days few parents would want to tell their child that masturbation is wrong or harmful, but still it is embarrassing if children do it whenever they are taken out visiting. In a case like this, the child should be told that it is perfectly all right to do it in her own bedroom, and that, if she wants to do it, then that or some other private place is where she should go. She should be praised for keeping to this idea. For the majority this will be enough; others might need simple preventative measures (wearing dungarees rather than trousers, or being given a special toy to fiddle with at danger times), and a low-key star-chart system – not for stopping the habit altogether, but for keeping it as a private pleasure.

References

1 P. A. Mahalski, 'The incidence of attachment objects and oral habits at bedtime in two longitudinal samples of children aged 1.5 to 7 years', *J. Child Psychol. Psychiatry*, 24 (1983), 283–95.
2 H. F. Harlow, 'The nature of love', *Am. Psychol.*, 13 (1958), 673–85.
3 D. W. Winnicott, *The Child, the Family and the Outside World*, Harmondsworth, Pelican, 1964.
4 D. Boniface and P. Graham, 'The three-year-old and his attachment to a special soft object', *J. Child Psychol. Psychiatry*, 20 (1979), 217–24.
5 J. Newson, E. Newson and P. A. Mahalski, 'Persistent infant comfort habits and their sequelae at 11 and 16 years', *J. Child Psychol. Psychiatry*, 23 (1982), 421–36.
6 H. Bakwin, 'Persistent finger-sucking in twins', *Dev. Med. Child Neurol.*, 13 (1971), 308–9.
7 M. Rutter, J. Tizard and K. Whitmore, *Education, Health and Behaviour*, London, Longmans, 1970.
8 M. Ozturk and O. M. Ozturk, 'Thumbsucking and falling asleep', *B. J. Med. Psychol.*, 50 (1977), 95–103.
9 A. S. Traisman and H. S. Traisman, 'Thumb and finger sucking: a study of 2650 infants and children', *J. Paediat.*, 52 (1958), 566–72.
10 A. F. Tryon, 'Thumb sucking and manifest anxiety: a note', *Child Dev.*, 39 (1968), 1159–63.
11 M. E. J. Curzon, 'Dental implications of thumb-sucking', *Paediatrics*, 54 (1974), 196–9.
12 H. Bakwin, 'Nail-biting in twins', *Dev. Med. Child Neurol.*, 13 (1971), 304–7.
13 D. M. Levy, 'Finger sucking and accessory movements in early infancy: an ethological study', *Amer. J. Psychiatry*, 7 (1928), 881–918.

13 Aggression

Many of the problem behaviours we have looked at so far are a problem only to the child himself and his family. Aggression is different. Aggression affects other people and, because the parents' reaction to it has to take into account the repercussions for others, it is a particularly sensitive and difficult issue to handle.

Individual differences in aggression

It does appear that some children are consistently more aggressive than others: research has shown that, next to intelligence, aggression is one of the most stable psychological traits over time.[1] Children who were most aggressive at three, for example, on one follow-up study,[2] were also the children who fought and quarrelled most at fourteen and on into early adulthood. Considerable research effort has gone into finding out what might be responsible for these consistent individual differences in aggression. Some of the factors isolated include:

● Being male. A variety of studies, spanning many age groups and cultures, has shown that the male is undoubtedly the more aggressive member of the human species, and much less inhibited than the female about causing physical hurt to others. A particularly vivid example comes from a classic study[3] where the subjects of the experiment (college students) were told they were to be research assistants in a learning experiment and asked to administer electric shocks to a learner whenever the learner made a mistake. There were in fact no shocks but the learner simulated pain. Women subjects more often refused to administer shock and characteristically gave lower levels of shock to the mock victim than did male subjects. With children it will come as no surprise at all to parents to learn that observations in school playgrounds in several countries show that boys are much more likely than girls to hit and shove; it may be more interesting to note that these sex differences can be traced as far back as the toddler years.[4]

- Temperament. Aggression was one feature of the disturbed behaviour shown in later years by the infants with a 'difficult' temperament in Thomas and Chess' New York Longitudinal Study.[5] The baby who early on is unmalleable, intense and predominantly negative in his emotions and irregular in his routines has an increased risk of becoming aggressive as he grows older. So, it appears, are the toddler and pre-school child who are very active and impulsive, always 'on the go'.[6] Whether these temperamental traits are linked directly with later aggression, or whether the link is mediated by the way the parent reacts to this active, awkward, negative behaviour pattern in their small child (see page 104), we are not yet entirely sure.

- Child-rearing practices involving harsh punishment, especially when combined with coldness and rejection.[7] The link between aggression and the excessive use of physical punishment was explored in chapter 6, along with the suggestion that parents who do smack a great deal are inadvertently providing their children with a model for aggressive behaviour. The physical-punishment issue, however, is secondary to the emotional climate in the home: in his extensive research in Sweden Dan Olweus[8] identified what he termed the 'silent violence' exerted by parents who are unable to show warmth to their children, and which has worse effects than physical violence alone. Olweus was studying teenage boys rated for aggression by their peers: in interviews with the boys' parents he found that the mother's negative feelings for her son in his early childhood had much to do with the later development of aggressive behaviour. He also noted, interestingly, how such negative feelings might arise: it was the boys who were hot-headed and active in the pre-school years whose mothers most often felt hostile towards them – an inevitable reaction, perhaps, to the strain of living with an exhausting child.

A permissive attitude towards aggression was another factor which Olweus identified as contributing to later aggressive behaviour. The mothers of the aggressive teenagers had never really been able to stop them showing aggression towards brothers and sisters, peers or the parents themselves. (This ties in with the research of Gerald Patterson and his colleagues who, as we saw in chapter 3, identified the parents of aggressive, difficult boys as unable to set 'house rules' and maintain clear limits.) The young boy, Olweus concludes, who gets 'too little love and interest from his principal caretaker, and too much freedom and lack of constraint with regard to aggressive behaviour, is particularly likely to develop into an aggressive adolescent.'

The child who *is* brought up in a warm and loving emotional climate can also show aggression, though of a rather different kind. If his parents are generally permissive, exert little control and are not persistent in enforcing their demands, he may end up impulsive and undisciplined, hitting out without thinking but without intending to hurt. He will not, however, show any real malice in his aggression, as may the conflicted, unhappy child of rejecting parents.

● Repeated experience of frustration. Aggressive, irritable behaviour most often occurs in response to frustration. Few parents need to be told this; it was neatly demonstrated, however, in another classic study[9] where two groups of children were shown a playroom full of desirable toys – one group was allowed to stay and play there, while the other was led away from the playroom and only allowed to return after a frustrating delay. The first group played constructively and co-operatively; the second broke the toys, quarrelled with each other and played much more aimlessly. Long-term frustrations may be the reason why, for example, children from divorced families often have problems with aggression – in a survey of American children those whose parents had recently divorced were more antagonistic and aggressive than others; over time these differences gradually decreased for girls, but the boys from divorced families were still more hostile two years after the divorce than other boys.[10] Amother long-term source of frustration is educational failure: such failure is common in the history of aggressive, difficult children. It is easy to guess how months and years spent struggling with school work, with no experience of success and few opportunities to earn praise in a system geared to the needs of the academically able, could provoke an increasingly angry reaction.

● Television violence. In the short term children *do* imitate television and film aggression they have observed: the evidence for this is now overwhelming.[4] In particular, children who are *already aggressive* are most influenced by TV violence. This was the finding in a study of nursery-school children[11] who were systematically observed over a four-week period, then shown one of the three types of TV programmes several times a week for a month – aggressive cartoons, 'prosocial' films depicting acts of kindness and co-operation, and neutral films. Children who were below the group average in their initial levels of aggression showed no significant increase after the aggressive films, but children initially above average in aggression were made much more aggressive by them.

In the longer term, there is also some evidence that television violence affects children: in one important study of Lefkowitz and associates[12] boys who at nine years showed a preference for watching violent TV programmes were more aggressive ten years later than a carefully matched group of boys who watched less violent material. Other studies, however, have not shown such clear-cut long-term effects,[4] and the issue remains open.

Implications

For the moment, until research proves otherwise, the parent who is concerned about a child's aggressive behaviour will probably want to keep him away from TV violence in any form; he will avoid modelling aggression by too much smacking; he will be firm by issuing relatively few directives to the child but making sure to follow through consistently on those he does issue. The parent will recognize the times when the child is most vulnerable to the effects of frustration – when he is tired, hungry, unwell – and avoid overtaxing him then. He or she will also avoid situations which are particularly likely to lead to immediate frustration (such as many children trying to share a small number of toys). Looking at long-term sources of frustration, and trying to remedy them, will be important but not always easy. Hardest of all may be trying to maintain a positive attitude to a small child who is awkward, obstinate, unpredictable and overactive: parents who do have a child like this should not be afraid to seek as much help and support as they can get from family, friends and possibly also from professionals.

Handling aggression: redirection?

Some children do seem to be helped if parents suggest ways of handling frustration that will not hurt others: having, for example, a special cushion or sag-bag or inflatable toy to take it out on when things are going badly. The actual evidence from psychological research, however, does not in general tend to support the effectiveness of such a redirection of aggression – or catharsis, as it is sometimes called. Expressing aggression only reduces further aggression if the expression is directed at the person one is angry with: an opportunity to get back at this other person *directly* does reduce systolic blood pressure and other measures of physiological arousal,[13] but kicking the cat may not do nearly so well. Indeed some widely advocated forms of catharsis (such as physical exercise and sport) have been shown to *increase* subsequent aggression rather than decrease it: increases in verbal and physical aggression have been found after boys were given the chance to engage in physical activities like rough-and-tumble play,[14] and committing aggressive acts in organized sports makes it more, not less likely, that the individual will engage in future aggression.[15] 'Letting off steam', in practice, does not seem to work. Nor are the quieter forms of competitive activity likely to use up stores of aggression either, as this experiment shows:[16]

A group of boys were asked to draw a picture of their school, for which they might, they were told, earn a prize if the picture were good enough. Half of the group were then artificially angered by being told that another boy had said their drawing was no good, so that they would not now win a prize. The angered subjects were given the chance of playing a competitive button-pushing game against the boy who had criticized their picture. The results of this game could be 'fixed' by the experimenter to make it look as if the angered subject had won or lost. After the game the angered subjects' aggression towards their 'critic' was measured by how far they would turn up the volume control when administering an unpleasant loud noise to let the other boy know he had made a mistake on some maths problems. It was found that the chance to play a competitive game against the other boy *increased* the aggression shown later towards him, particularly if the previously angered boy was led to believe he had *won* the competitive game. Beating an adversary, far from using up anger, seemed to reinforce or reward the angry child in his attempts to get even, and it made future aggression more rather than less likely.

Teaching alternatives to aggression

Rewarding co-operation is one very potent way of reducing aggression: unlike catharsis, it has actually been shown to work. In one well-known study in a nursery school,[17] for example, teachers were able to *halve* the rate of fights and squabbles simply by paying attention to the children when they were playing peacefully, with comments like 'That's nice', 'You *are* playing well together', 'No fighting, that's very good, well done'. In situations where praise alone is not enough, many parents, seriously worried about their child's inability to play without fighting, have had success with star-chart systems: if the child can manage to have a friend over for an hour with no fights, he sticks on a star, five stars being exchangeable for a special treat like having a friend to stay the night or accompany the family on an outing. To cover aggression at school, a contract can be drawn up between the child, his teachers and parents, on lines like these:

> I, John Smith, agree that I will try not to get into fights in the playground.
> For every playtime without fighting or hitting I will receive one point.
> When I have twelve points, I can exchange them for either half an hour
> on the school computer, *or* going to a football match with my Dad, *or* a
> hamburger at MacDonalds.

Reward systems like these may not work if the child does not know what else to do, other than hit or fight, in conflict situations. Here the parents of younger children can help by sitting down with them and enacting with dolls or small figures some common sources of conflict and the various ways in which they can be handled: a toy rabbit starts a fight with a cat over the ball they both want, and both get hurt, or the same toy rabbit says 'Can I have it

after you?', 'Do you want to play football with me?' (or a similar
turn-taking/sharing remark) with a demonstrated happy ending. This kind
of modelling has been found in experiments to work well with pre-school
children.[18]

Children of all ages can benefit from learning how to assert themselves in
non-violent ways: how to say 'no', how to react if hit or threatened by another
child. Assertiveness training is described in chapter 15, along with what the
psychologists who developed them call 'problem-solving techniques'. These
are techniques which aim to get the child to look at conflict from several
viewpoints, to think of many different ways of tackling it, and to evaluate the
consequences of each possibility. A typical problem-solving conversation
about an act of aggression might go like this:

> *Parent:* How did David feel when you hit him?
> *Child:* Angry . . . he told the teacher.
> *Parent:* What did you hit him for?
> *Child:* 'Cos he wouldn't lend me his rubber.
> *Parent:* Do you know why he wouldn't? How can you find out?
> *Child:* I could ask him . . . he says I lost the last one.
> *Parent:* Now you know more about what happened. Can you think of
> anything else you could have done or said so he would lend you his
> rubber?
> *Child:* I could say I wouldn't play with him.
> *Parent:* What would happen then?
> *Child:* He wouldn't be my friend.
> *Parent:* Do you want him to be your friend?
> *Child:* Yes . . . I could let him have a go with my car at playtime if he lent
> me the rubber.
> *Parent:* That's another idea. Any more?
> *Child:* I could get him one instead of the one that got lost. I could pay for
> it. I'll try that.

All the strategies described in this section share a *positive* approach to
teaching the child about alternatives to aggression. It is not enough, as with
other kinds of misbehaviour, simply to ignore aggressive behaviour, to 'let
them sort it out for themselves'. Left to themselves, without adult
intervention, a group of children will become *more* aggressive over time
rather than less: aggression has its own rewards which tend to keep it going.
For example, Patterson and his colleagues,[6] observing children in nursery
schools, found that eighty per cent of the aggressive behaviour observed had
some positive pay-off for the aggressor: the victim gave up a toy, or cried or
ran away. Other children soon began to imitate their more aggressive peers
and one successful hit or shove was enough to start a previously
non-aggressive child off on a whole series. Aggression does demand an adult
intervention of an *active* kind.

Time out

Research suggests that by far the most effective intervention is for the adult to apply time out, the technique described in chapter 7.[19] To ignore aggression is, as we have seen, not a good idea. To smack the child hardly helps get across the non-violent message. To scold him, or reason with him there and then, risks maintaining the aggressive behaviour by giving it attention. Later in the day there should be a time to discuss the situation and apply reasoning and problem-solving techniques; the immediate situation, however, requires that the child be removed – calmly and without comment – from any possible rewarding consequences of his aggression. Two to five minutes in whichever room or spot you have chosen as the least interesting in the house are all that is needed. If you are not at home, try to find some other way of isolating the child temporarily from the group – on a chair with his back to the others, outside the room, in the car with you standing nearby. Simply preventing the young child from playing, while allowing him to watch the other children at play, may be enough: one group of investigators[20] tried this method (removing the aggressor from play for a period of one minute only) in a nursery school, comparing it with the more usual method of telling the child not to hit and redirecting him to other play. The removal-from-play technique was much more successful than traditional scolding and redirection. A variant on the technique, which also seems to work well,[21] is making a big fuss of the *victim* while the aggressor looks on. Logical consequences can be used, too, if the child is old enough and it is possible for you to leave the scene of the aggression: 'You don't yet know how to play without fighting, so we will have to go home now and try again another time.' It is important to remember that logical consequences are never to be used as an empty threat ('If you don't stop, we'll go home') and must be carried out if they are to be effective.

If they seem laborious, the techniques of time out, logical consequences, contracts and star charts are in practice very easy to use and very much less emotionally wearing on the parent than many more usual reactions to children's aggression. The parent need not, either, fear that they will need to be used for ever. What they do is break an aggressive habit and push the child into less easy but more satisfying alternatives of compromise, sharing, turn-taking and negotiation. These have their own built-in reward for the child: an increase in popularity. Research has shown that the children most often rejected by their peers are the ones who show a great deal of unprovoked physical and verbal aggression.[22] If the parent can help the child break the aggressive habit, his new friends will do the job of maintaining co-operative behaviour. The parents will need only once in a while to praise him for his efforts to hold on to his temper and keep from hitting out.

References

1 D. Olweus, 'Stability of aggressive reaction patterns in males: a review', *Psychol. Bull.*, 86 (1979), 852–75.
2 J. Kagan and H. Moss, *From Birth to Maturity*, New York, John Wiley, 1962.
3 S. Milgram, *Obedience to Authority*, New York, Harper and Row, 1974.
4 D. Schaffer, H. F. L. Meyer-Bahlburg and C. L. J. Stokman, 'The development of aggression' in M. Rutter (ed.), *Scientific Foundations of Developmental Psychiatry*, London, Heinemann Medical Books, 1980.
5 A. Thomas, S. Chess and H. Birch, *Temperament and Behaviour in Children*, New York, University Press, 1965.
6 G. R. Patterson, R. A. Littman and W. Bricker, 'Assertive behaviour in children: a step toward a theory of aggression', *Monog. Soc. Res. Child Dev.*, 32 (1967) no. 5.
7 W. C. Becker, 'Consequences of different kinds of parental discipline', in M. L. Hoffman and L. W. Hoffman (eds), *Review of Child Development Research*, vol. 1, Russell Sage Foundation, 1962, 161–208.
8 D. Olweus, 'Bullies and the bullied', in N. Frude and H. Gault (eds), *Disruptive Behaviour in Schools*, London, Wiley, 1984.
9 R. Barker, T. Dembo and K. Lewin, 'Frustration and aggression. An experiment with young children', *University of Iowa Studies in Child Welfare*, 18 (1941), 1–34.
10 E. M. Hetherington, M. Cox and R. Cox, 'Effects of divorce on parents and children', in M. E. Lamb (ed.), *Non-traditional Families*, Hillside, New Jersey, Lawrence Erlbaum, 1982.
11 L. K. Friedrich and A. H. Stein, 'Aggressive and prosocial television programmes and the natural behaviour of preschool children', *Monog. Soc. Res. Child Dev.*, 38 (1973), no. 151.
12 M. M. Lefkowitz, L. D. Eron, L. O. Walder and L. R. Huesmann, *Growing up to be violent: a Longitudinal Study of the Development of Aggression*, New York, Pergamon Press, 1977.
13 J. E. Hokanson and M. Burgess, 'The effects of three types of aggression on vascular processes', *J. Abn. Soc. Psychol.*, 64 (1962), 446–9.
14 R. Geen and M. Quanty, 'The catharsis of aggression: an evaluation of a hypothesis', in L. Berkowitz (ed.), *Advances in Experimental Social Psychology*, vol. 10, New York, Academic Press, 2–37.
15 L. Berkowitz, *Aggression: a Social Psychological Analysis*, New York, McGraw-Hill, 1962.
16 D. G. Perry and L. C. Perry, 'A note on the effects of prior anger arousal and winning or losing a competition on aggressive behaviour in boys', *J. Child Psychol. Psychiatry*, 17 (1976), 145–9.
17 P. Brown and R. Elliott, 'Control of aggression in a nursery school class', *J. Exptal. Child Psychol.*, 2 (1965), 103–7.
18 G. E. Chittenden, 'An experimental study in measuring and modifying assertive behaviour in young children', *Monog. Soc. Res. Child Dev.*, 7 (1942), no. 1.
19 F. Frankel and J. Q. Simmons, 'Behavioural treatment approaches to pathological unsocialized physical aggression in young children', *J. Child Psychol. Psychiatry*, 26 (1985), 525–51.
20 J. K. Porterfield, E. Herbert-Jackson and T. R. Risley, 'Contingent observation:

an effective and acceptable procedure for reducing disruptive behaviour of young children in a group setting', *J. Applied Behav. Analysis*, 9 (1976), 44–55.

21 E. M. Pinkston, N. M. Reese, J. M. LeBlanc and D. M. Baer, 'Independent control of a preschool child's aggression and peer interaction by contingent teacher attention', *J. Applied Behav. Analysis*, 6 (1973), 115–24.

22 E. Hartup, 'Peer interaction and social organization', in P. H. Mussen (ed.), *Carmichael's Manual of Child Psychology*, vol. 2, New York, Wiley, 1970.

14 Brothers and sisters

The area where parents would often most like to see peaceful, co-operative behaviour, and the area where they are usually least likely to see it, is in the relationship between siblings. Handling sibling quarrels is a major issue; it takes up a lot of time for many parents who find themselves uneasily combining roles of arbitrator, judge and referee for much of the typical family day. Sorting out who said what to whom, who started it, who went too far, who did it and why is a habitual occupation for many of us. We assume that it is necessary and useful. Psychological research is beginning now to try and find out if this assumption is correct. It is trying also to answer the question of why some children in a family are good friends, while others do nothing but fight; it is asking whether jealousy and quarrels are really – as many childcare manuals suggest – the fault of the parents and, if not, what other factors could be responsible.

Jealousy

Few parents nowadays are unaware of the depth of jealousy a young child very often feels for a new arrival in the family. Many will have heard that particularly useful analogy in which the child's feelings about the birth of a sibling are compared to those the parent might have if the spouse announced that he or she was bringing home a new wife or husband – '. . . and I know you're both going to be good company for each other, and get on really well.' It is to Freud and his followers[1] that we owe our ability to acknowledge that a child does have a very intense bond with her primary caretaker, a feeling of being part of a couple, and that she will find it hard to understand why the parents should want to disrupt this bond and (to her mind) replace her with another.

Other psychological theories offer different explanations of jealousy between brothers and sisters but still stress that it is inevitable and universal. In learning theory the presence of the sibling is regularly and repeatedly paired with a withdrawal or reduction of parental attention to the child herself. This repeated pairing establishes the brother or sister as a 'conditioned stimulus', or signal, that the mother or father is going to be less available. Increasingly the mere sight of the sibling will come to evoke angry and resentful feelings.

However we interpret them, we know that such feelings are very common indeed. People who interview young children have found that they use far more emotional words to describe their brothers and sisters than to describe friends or even parents, and that more often than not (in about two-thirds of cases) the words are negative.[2] One-third of five- and six-year-olds in one study said they would prefer to be without their sibling altogether.[3] Quarrels are frequent: two-thirds of a sample of Nottingham seven-year-olds[4] fought sometimes or often with their siblings, and half of these (girls as well as boys) actually came to blows fairly regularly. .

The frequency of adverse reactions to the birth of a new baby in the family has been documented by Judy Dunn and her associates in Cambridge who are currently the leading authorities world-wide on the sibling relationship. What the Cambridge group did, in one of the first of their studies, was to observe the behaviour of the older child (aged between eighteen months and forty-three months) over the weeks immediately after the arrival of a sibling, in a large group of families.[5] Mothers were also interviewed. The majority of the children did show signs of disturbance: tearfulness, defiance, demanding or clinging behaviour, lapses in toilet training and sleep problems. Most of these problems had disappeared by the time the new baby was eight months old, with the exception of fearful, anxious behaviour which tended to persist.

In follow-up studies these same families were seen again when the older child was three, and when she was six. A high degree of consistency was found in the way the older child felt about the sibling. The first-borns who had shown a good deal of positive interest in the new baby in the weeks after the birth were more likely to make positive comments about the sibling when interviewed as six-year-olds; brothers and sisters who got on well when the first-born was three were also more likely to get on well three years later. Good or bad feeling between siblings seemed to start early, and to persist.

The usual explanation, as Judy Dunn points out,[6] why some siblings feel good about each other, and others don't, is in terms of factors like birth order, age gap and the sex of the children. Many parents, for instance, carefully plan their families so that, they hope, the children will be close enough in age to be friends . . . or far enough apart to each get a good share of attention . . . or whatever their experience of their own and others' families has led them to believe. In fact, there is remarkably little evidence, according to the Cambridge group, that any of these things matter as much as we might think. For example, although we feel intuitively that a first-born child is more likely to be jealous by virtue of being displaced than is her younger brother or sister, research has *not* found that first-borns in practice express any less warmth and affection for their siblings than the later-borns. Birth order does affect *how* the child handles disputes within the family:[7] first-borns use more domineering verbal tactics and bribes, whereas the later-borns are more physically aggressive and also sulk/pout/plead/cry and appeal more to the parents for help. But it does not seem to affect the quality of the sibling relationship as such.

On the age-gap question there are contradictory findings.[6] Some studies report that there are more quarrels and conflict in children close together in age (less than two years apart). Others find most conflict with a two-to-four year gap. In her own research Judy Dunn found *no* relationship between age gap (with gaps ranging from one to five years) and the number of quarrels between children,[8] nor between age gap and the amount of joint play, companionship and affection. The amount of positive interest in a new baby shown by the older child immediately after the birth was equally unrelated to age gap, although the *way* in which the first-born reacts to a new baby does vary with age: toddlers tend to become more tearful and clinging while three-to-four-year-olds become more naughty and defiant.[5]

As for gender differences between siblings, it does seem that when both children are young (under five), opposite-sexed siblings often show more antagonism towards each other than pairs of the same sex.[6] With older children we are less sure what happens. Boy–boy and girl–girl pairs continue to have more in common and play together more: in this sense they are close. At the same time competition and one-upmanship can be greater in same-sexed pairs. The relationship can go either way. Much depends on how 'closeness' between siblings is defined and measured; whether, for example, two children who play little together and therefore quarrel less are seen as closer than a pair who play, and fight, with each other for much of the day.

It is clear that, at least until we have sorted out such issues, neither birth order nor age gap nor gender allow us to predict in any consistent way which brothers and sisters will get on well together, and which won't. What, then, will? The respective temperaments of the children will obviously be important; this has been little researched, but we do know that children with low self-esteem are often very jealous of their siblings,[2] and that children with intense emotions and mainly negative mood react worse to the birth of a new baby than the more malleable, easy-going types.[5] Another important factor is the kind of relationship each child has with the parents. If the eldest child has had a very close, playful and loving relationship with the mother, and especially if this child is a girl, she will react with a lot of jealousy to a new baby and they are likely to get on badly together as the baby grows up. Much the same goes for the relationship with fathers.[5] Basically it seems that the more important the parents are to the child, the more she will resent a newcomer.

If, on the other hand, the parent–child relationship is more detached and less positive, then friendly relationships between the siblings become *more* likely. In families where the mother has been depressed after the second child's birth, for example, and has not been able to be very responsive to either child, the siblings often become very close and friendly,[5] as they also may in large families where the parents have a more diluted relationship with all their children.

No one would want to suggest that parents avoid closeness with one child so that she will get on better with her brothers and sisters. Jealousy, it seems, may be something the family has to live with: one of those powerful feelings that, even as adults, can surprise us with its intense and irrational qualities – intense and irrational just because its roots lie in our childhood experiences. Jealousy is part of growing up. Only if one child in the family is consistently preferred by the parents or is conspicuously more capable and successful than the others will the experience of jealousy be damaging.

Promoting good relationships

Since the majority of siblings do experience conflict, and since the conflict may be particularly marked in families where there have been close, warm parent–child relationships, it would clearly be wrong for parents to blame themselves if their children do not get on well. It may be, however, that the same research which releases parents from responsibility for their children's jealousy can also suggest positive steps they can take to promote better sibling relationships: practical steps to reduce inevitable conflict to manageable proportions.

Most child-care manuals are full of advice, most very sensible, on getting off to a good start when introducing a child first to the idea and then to the reality of a new baby in the family. It is not intended to repeat such advice in any great detail. Some of the Cambridge group's research-based suggestions on what to do when a new baby arrives are, however, well worth emphasizing. Dunn and her associates stress that it is important to keep changes in the older child's life to a minimum; that as far as possible she should keep to her old routine; and that the parents should try to keep constant the amount of play and attention she has been used to from them.

Dunn's finding that a close, positive relationship with the *father* before the birth of a sibling helps to reduce the amount of mother–child conflict in the weeks after the birth suggests how a father can help, by making himself increasingly available to the older child both before and after the new baby arrives. Both parents should expect the older child to show some disturbance after the birth, and remember that the problems of toileting, sleep, clinging and so on which she may show are generally transient. They can promote good feeling between the child and a baby brother or sister by drawing on another result from the Cambridge research: that siblings were particularly friendly over the next year in families where the mothers involved the older child in helping to care for the new baby, and particularly where the mother discussed with the older child what the baby might be feeling or needing and what they should do about it. Questions and suggestions like 'Do you think she's hungry?', 'What shall we do with her?', 'Can you talk to her and cheer her up?', 'Do you think she likes her bath?', 'See how she likes it when you make faces at her' seemed to help by making the older child acknowledge the baby as a person with wants and needs and feelings, right from the beginning. Lastly, Dunn's research suggests something to avoid: if the mother responded in a punitive way to the older child's negative reactions to the baby, jealousy was more likely to persist. Being angry with a jealous child is not likely to help her to learn to cope.

As yet unproven, but more likely to help such a child is the kind of listening to feelings by the parent which was described in chapter 9. Communication which reflects back to the child her anger and jealousy can be used at any age; not just when the child and her sibling are small. At four or fourteen, when the children are quarrelling, competing for attention or claiming 'It's not fair', you can say things like:

'I know sometimes you feel very angry with your brother.'

'He really bothers you, doesn't he?'

'Perhaps you feel a bit left out when I'm reading to Jane.'

'Sometimes you feel it was better before the baby was born.'

This kind of statement will let the child know you accept the way she feels, and that she has a right to feel that way – that there is no law that says we have to like our brothers and sisters. It should also aim at giving the child a better understanding of *why* she finds the brother and sister so hard to get on with: that the irrational hatred which she feels from time to time springs from having to share a very important relationship:

'Sometimes you'd like to have me all to yourself.'

'I wonder if you want to be sure I love you both the same.'

'It's very hard to share mummy, isn't it?'

All feelings are easier to handle if we know where they come from. Children's feelings are no exception to the rule.

Many parents might want to add to this kind of reflective listening some explanation to the child about their ability to love all their children equally, on the lines that love is not a finite quantity and that it can grow so there is enough for everybody. We should perhaps ask ourselves, however, whether such an explanation would help if a husband and wife tried it when explaining an extra-marital affair. Again, it comes back to our willingness to acknowledge that children's possessiveness is just as great as our own.

Sharing parental affection can be made a little easier if each child is allocated her own 'special time': fifteen minutes a day, perhaps, when she can choose to do something with either parent and be sure of being uninterrupted by brothers and sisters. Each child in the family should have her own special possessions and a small piece of private territory which the others are taught to respect – a high shelf, or a lockable cupboard: an area where she can make the kind of collections of favourite things by which we all define our uniqueness and identity. This helps, too, when friends come to play: any new or particularly special toy the child doesn't want to share can be put in the private territory. If an older child can't play the kinds of games she wants to – do a jigsaw puzzle or construct a Lego battleship – because of a younger brother or sister at the 'into everything' stage, the older child can work at a table or take her toys *inside* the playpen while the toddler stays outside. Logical consequences can and should be applied: if the older child knows her brother will break up a model left on the floor, and she still leaves it there, that is her problem and not the parents'.

Parents do not need to be told to be fair when dealing with their children; the children will soon complain loudly if they are not. On the whole, what is given to one should be given to all and usually is. Sometimes, however, this is carried to extremes; there are many families with not one, but two identical and extremely expensive galactic castles, doll's dream homes, or whatever – simply because the parents pursued fairness too far. These are often families where one or more children are very skilled at applying negative consequences if they don't get their own way: at tantrums, sulks, whines and carefully engineered sibling quarrels.

Being fair does not mean treating children exactly the same, at all times. Children are quite capable of understanding that if John is given a galactic castle and they are given the galactic garage, both will benefit if they are able to join forces and play together – more so than if there are two castles and no garage in the house. They are also able to understand that routines and rules vary with age. They can accept that being the eldest in a family confers certain privileges (like staying up half an hour later than the younger ones) but that these privileges are balanced by responsibilities (like helping to clear the table) which the younger children may not yet have to take on. The more clearly defined are the privileges and responsibilities, the easier this will be.

A final aspect of promoting good relationships between siblings concerns the parents' willingness to reward co-operation and harmony. The usual pattern in most families is for the parents to pay attention to the children when they quarrel but to pay much less attention when they are playing peacefully together. This is the time when most parents retreat gratefully to the kitchen to get on with the dinner. Several psychological studies,[9] however, have shown that paying attention to co-operative behaviours such as playing together, answering each other's questions and saying 'please' and 'thank you' can substantially increase the frequency of such behaviours. Comments like 'It is nice to see you do that jigsaw together', or 'No quarrels – that's wonderful' are easy to think of, and easy to make.

For most children such praise will improve the relationship. Getting on well with a sibling is, however, a very high-cost behaviour and may need to be balanced with a stronger reward: a few sweets handed out when a pair are playing well, or points, or stars on a chart. Dramatic results can be achieved this way:

> Rebecca, aged eight, had always been very jealous of her younger sister, Natalie, who was five. Natalie was not so jealous and often tried to join in her sister's play. She usually found the door shut against her or had to play minor parts like baby or servant in pretend games. Eventually she would object to this and there would be a quarrel. The girls bickered a great deal in a minor way, particularly when they had to sit close to each other as in the back of the car or while watching television. Their mother bought a tin of Quality Street – a rare family treat. The girls were promised a sweet each if they could manage not to quarrel for a whole morning, or a whole afternoon. To everyone's surprise, they earned their reward nine times out of ten and moved on to a sweet for a whole day without quarrelling. At the end of the tin, the rewards stopped. The girls continued, however, to quarrel very little: they could be heard negotiating, taking turns and reaching compromises, and seemed to have learned on a permanent basis some different ways of handling disagreements. Three months later the improvement was still very noticeable.

Quarrels: to intervene or not to intervene

There is some debate among psychologists about the issue of parental intervention in their children's disputes. Some stress that parental attention inadvertently rewards quarrelling, and that quarrelling will continue so long as each child has the chance of seeing the other scolded, and of winning – albeit temporarily – the parent's favour. Others argue that parental intervention is necessary to teach concepts of fair play and conciliation. Many parents feel, too, that if they *don't* intervene, injustice will be done (particularly to the younger and weaker child), and that they will be condoning aggression or tyranny.

Judy Dunn is one of the few investigators who have attempted to provide some hard evidence on the effects of stepping in to sort out arguments. In a recent report,[8] she reviews several studies in which parents were trained to stay right out of sibling quarrels, and in which the frequency of such arguments was shown to decline – particularly if ignoring quarrels was combined with rewarding 'no conflict' as in the case of Rebecca and Natalie above. On the other hand, she points out, other research has shown that in order to help young children develop an ability to care about what happens to other people, parents need to point out to them very clearly and forcefully the consequences of being unkind and aggressive – and that quarrels between brothers and sisters are the prime ground for this kind of teaching.

Dunn and her co-worker Penny Munn directly observed what went on between siblings in their own homes, in forty-three sibling pairs where the younger child was eighteen months old. They went back six months later for further observation. The mothers' behaviour was also recorded. The findings were fascinating. First, there was a lot of quarrelling – about eight fights, or potential fights, per hour on average. Second, it did seem that the mother's intervention in quarrels *increased* conflict in the long term: in families where the mother tended to intervene often in the first observation period, the children had longer quarrels and more physical fights six months later, in the second observation period, than in families where she intervened less. However, there was also evidence that a maternal style of discussing rules and feelings with the children when they quarrelled led to the development of more mature ways of handling conflict – such as conciliation (where the child shows concern for, comforts, helps or apologizes to the other) and reference to rules ('We have to take turns, mummy said so').

How can we resolve the contradictory implications of this research? In many ways the contradictions resemble those we have met before in this book: that reasoning with children and helping them develop an awareness of others' feelings promote the development of conscience and resistance to temptation, while at the same time reasoning with them means giving them a great deal of attention which might reward and maintain misbehaviour. The best bet again appears to be an 'act now – talk later' strategy: ignore the quarrel at the time, but get both children together later on and discuss how each felt and how they might have resolved their differences. Ignoring quarrels at the time will be particularly important if you suspect your children fight more when you are around; there is some evidence for this,[10] as we would expect if we assume that at least some arguments are bids for attention or the parent's favour.

There is one exception to this strategy: physical aggression in a sibling quarrel. This should *not* be ignored. It has been shown by several investigators[11] that, if the parent permits such physical aggression between siblings at home, their children are much more likely to act aggressively outside the home, for example, at nursery school. The parents need to make it clear that while he or she is not interested in hearing about arguments, or in tale-telling, or in being a referee, he or she will not allow hitting or hurting. If there is any hitting or hurting, both children will spend five minutes in separate time out: on chairs facing the wall in different rooms, or in upstairs bathroom and downstairs cloakroom or wherever.

Why both children? Consider these situations:

> Sam, aged four, was sitting next to Ben, his seven-year-old brother, watching television. He was not particularly interested in the programme and began to bounce up and down, annoying Ben who *was* interested in it. Ben told him to sit still. Sam went on bouncing. Ben shouted at him to stop: 'I want to watch this.' Sam bounced some more. Finally Ben turned round and thumped him: Sam shrieked and his mother rushed in: 'Whatever's the matter?' she asked Sam. 'He kept on bothering me,' said Ben. 'I've told you before *not* to hit him; you're a very naughty boy. Go to your room,' said the mother. Sam looked pleased.

> Five-year-old Jane was in the car with her older brother, Paul. She decided to spread herself a little and put her feet up on the seat so that she was touching Paul. Very gently, she nudged him with her foot. He pushed her away. Jane tried again, and again. Paul pinched her, hard, on the calf. Jane burst into tears. 'Daddy, he pinched me,' she sobbed. Daddy turned round and yelled at Paul: 'You great bully . . . you're always hurting Jane . . . pick on someone your own size.'

Events like these are not uncommon; it does take two to make a quarrel, and subtle provocation by a younger child, so that he or she will be fussed over and big brother/sister told off, can be observed in many families. It is a well-documented fact that mothers have a tendency to side with their younger children, and that this is not always justified. Dunn, for example,[5] reports that two-year-old second-born children were *just* as likely as their older siblings to start a quarrel, to tease, and to hit. But their mothers were *twice* as likely to scold the older child and tell her to stop; they tended with the younger child not to scold but to distract her and try to get her interested in something other than the source of conflict.[8]

Responsibility for disputes is likely, in any family, to shift: half the time one child may have 'started it', half the time the other. Applying the same consequences to both of them not only relieves the parent from the elaborate detective work needed to choose a culprit, but also teaches the children that they need to co-operate in resolving conflict.

A similar strategy can be used when the children are arguing over a toy: the parent takes the toy from *both* of them and puts it firmly out of reach. On just one occasion this might be unfair to whichever child had the toy first, but over several occasions the unfairness evens out. The children soon learn that they either work out some way of sharing and turn-taking, or no one will have the chance to play with the toy. It is, after all, a logical consequence: 'If you can't sort this out between you, then it is better if no one has it.' Arguments over which television programmes to watch can soon be resolved if the parent switches off the television when the children can't agree: 'There's no way you can both have what you want here, so you will both need to find something else to do.'

Summarizing this approach to quarrels, intervention is definitely necessary for physical aggression, and intervention in the form of taking away the object of dispute from *both* children (when there is such a focus to their quarrel) can be very effective. Otherwise quarrels should be ignored. If one child comes to tell you about a dispute, she should be told: 'I'm not interested in quarrels.' This serves the added purpose of avoiding bringing up the kind of child who is forever saying 'I'm telling on you' – something heard often from the younger child; this might be a legitimate means of self-defence but more often becomes another way in which she provokes and taunts her elders.

Using strategies like these, parents can reduce the amount their children quarrel. They will never get rid of the conflicts completely, nor perhaps should they want to. Surprisingly, many positive things are learned from those arguments. Psychologists have long stressed the importance of the brother–sister relationship as a safe setting in which to learn how to manage feelings of hatred and rivalry. Through very close daily contact with brothers and sisters, children learn how to anticipate other people's behaviour, and how to understand another's point of view. They have an opportunity – not available in play with friends – to take on protective or dominating roles, and to practise being a follower. The origins of our concepts of justice, and fairness, are thought also to be found in the sibling relationship. That relationship may, to the weary parents, sometimes seem like a battle-ground, but it is a battle-ground where the opponents learn a great deal and come to no lasting harm.

References

1 C. Dare, 'Psychoanalytic theories of development', in M. Rutter and L. Hersov (eds), *Child and Adolescent Psychiatry*, 2nd edn., Oxford, Blackwell Scientific Publications, 1985.

2 R. Stillwell, 'Social relationships in primary school children as seen by children, mothers and teachers', unpublished doctoral dissertation, University of Cambridge, 1984.

3 H. L. Koch, 'The relation of certain formal attributes of siblings to attitudes held toward each other and toward their parents', *Monog. of Soc. Res. Child Dev.*, 25 (1960), no. 4.

4 J. Newson and E. Newson, *Seven Years Old in the Home Environment*, Harmondsworth, Penguin, 1976.
5 J. Dunn and C. Kendrick, *Siblings: Love, Envy and Understanding*, Cambridge, Mass., Harvard University Press, 1982.
6 J. Dunn, *Sisters and Brothers*, London, Fontana, 1984.
7 B. Sutton-Smith and B. G. Rosenberg, *The Sibling*, New York, Holt, Rinehart and Winston, 1970.
8 J. Dunn and P. Munn, 'Sibling quarrels and maternal intervention: individual differences in understanding and aggression', *J. Child Psychol. Psychiatry*, 27 (1986), 583–95.
9 G. H. Brody and Z. Stoneman, 'Children with atypical siblings', in B. B. Lahey and A. E. Kazdin (eds), *Advances in Clinical Child Psychology*, vol. 6, Plenum Press, 1983.
10 E. J. Marsh and B. J. Mercer, 'A comparison of the behaviour of deviant and non-deviant boys while playing alone and interacting with a sibling, *J. Child Psychol. Psychiatry*, 20 (1979), 197–207.
11 G. R. Patterson, R. A. Littman and W. Bricker, 'Assertive behaviour in children: a step toward a theory of aggression', *Monog. Soc. Res. Child Dev.*, 32 (1967), no. 5.

15 Children's friendships

Friends matter to all of us, to children, perhaps, more even than they do to adults. Adults can make do at a pinch with family, work and interests; children of school age find themselves daily in a social situation they cannot avoid. They must either make friends or feel rejected and left out. Their happiness, as every parent knows, is very closely linked with how well, or how badly, their friendships are going at the time. A child with a friend, or a group of friends, is a happy child. A child who is even temporarily without a friend will almost always be sad, though he may not show it directly. Parents watching their child experiencing problems with his peer group, will want to offer support but will often feel particularly powerless and at a loss. If there is any information which could help them to help the child make and keep friends or cope with teasing and bullying and feeling left out, they will want to know about it. In this chapter we will look at such information: at research into what makes some children popular and others not, and at the attempts which psychologists and other social scientists are increasingly making to teach children friendship skills.

Stages in friendship

How soon in his life can a child be expected to have a real friend? A few years ago most texts on child development put the capacity for friendship (involving co-operation, turn-taking, a special responsiveness of a pair of friends towards each other) quite late in the developmental sequence. Not until around three and a half, it was thought, could children truly co-operate in play. Before that, they went through stages of solitary play and 'looking on' at other children's activities, parallel play (using the same toys as other children nearby but each child playing his own separate game), and then associative play (playing the same game, such as chasing one another, but without the division of labour which later makes each child able to take a role in games like doctors and nurses or mothers and fathers). Associative play was observed most in the two-to-three-year age group; parallel play usually began after twenty months; solitary and onlooker play before twenty months.[1]

More recent research, however, has shown – as many mothers would confirm – that even at the toddler stage children can form friendships that are very important to them, *if* they have the chance to play with the same child regularly. Judith Rubenstein and Carollee Howes,[2] in the USA, watched the play of eight pairs of nineteen-month-old children who knew each other well and had visited each other's homes two or three times a week for some months. These toddlers spent a good proportion of the time in joint games; they imitated and offered toys to each other; they were much more interested in their 'friend' than in their mother during the visit; they played more creatively with their toys when the friend was there than when they were alone.

Friendships, then, can begin early when parents provide the right conditions. A pair is the most likely form of early friendship; in the second year of life children tend to interact in twos even if they are in larger groups (such as 'mother and toddlers'). By the age of three, the twosomes often become threesomes, and by the time they leave nursery school or playgroup we find children regularly playing in stable groups with up to five members.[3] In the school years boys continue to prefer groups, while girls pair off with displays of intimacy (holding hands, sharing secrets) and of jealousy if one or other in the pair finds another friend. Friendships, whether group or pair, become more and more stable as adolescence approaches; at one extreme in the preschool years a best friend is often a thing of the moment, a matter of 'whoever I happen to be playing with at the time' as we saw in chapter 10, while at the other extreme the friends we make as teenagers are often friends for life. Real friendship between the sexes is rare between the nursery school years (when children first show a definite preference for playmates of their own sex) and adolescence: boys and girls in the eight-to-twelve range are intensely interested in sexual matters and do begin to show romantic attachments of a sort, but as Zick Rubin points out in his recent book on children and friends,[4] their relationships are 'strained' and based on teasing, hints and indirect messages (of the 'John really likes you' type) rather than any real communication or conversation. This becomes more possible in the teenage years as the same-sex pairs or small groups give way to larger mixed-sex groups from which boy–girl pairs gradually split off and go their own way.

The popular child

Research on the question of what makes for popularity usually begins by asking each child in a class or group to nominate (privately, and in confidence) the three or so other children in the class he likes best or would choose to play/work with. An alternative technique is to ask the child to rate every other group member on a points scale according to a criterion such as 'How much do you like to play with this child?' With pre-school children, direct observation takes the place of ratings, and the number of times a child is 'approached' by others, for example, can be recorded.

Using this kind of direct observation in a day-care centre, Lee C. Lee[5] was able to show that some children are 'popular' and others 'unpopular' very early indeed – nine months was the average age of the group in this study. Even at this age, one baby was consistently approached most often by all the others, and another was consistently avoided. The 'popular' baby was emotionally responsive, always reacted when approached and rarely rejected social overtures. The unpopular baby was only interested in 'interaction' if he had started it; he wouldn't give up even if he was getting no response; he was rough and tended to grab; he rarely smiled or laughed if another baby approached him.

In nursery schools, studies have found that popularity depends on how much the child dispenses 'social rewards' to his peers.[6] The popular pre-schoolers were those who said approving things to other children, who comforted them if they were hurt, who helped them if they needed help, and who tended to submit and acquiesce to what was asked of them. The unpopular children were those who tended to be physically aggressive, to insult and ridicule others, and to be unwilling to go along with their suggestions.

A word of caution is needed here; we should not necessarily assume from findings like these that popularity is a consequence of being nice to others. It could equally be the case that popularity *causes* a child to be happier and more kindly disposed to others, or that some third factor (being brought up in a stable, loving home, say) 'causes' both popularity and kindliness – so that the original two factors are not causally related at all. In fact, however, there is some research in which children have been directly taught how to be more rewarding to others and in which their popularity has subsequently been shown to increase,[7] and this research does tend to substantiate the not unreasonable notion that being nice to other people makes them like us more. In all probability what we have here is a circular reaction: the child who is nice to others becomes popular, and his positive experiences then lead him to be ever nicer and more socially rewarding, while the child who is aggressive and unkind becomes unpopular, and his experiences of feeling left out and lonely lead him to be ever nastier and less rewarding.

A similar circularity probably applies also to another finding, this time with eight- and nine-year-old children, that popularity is associated with 'social knowledge' – knowing *how to go about* the business of making contact with others. In this study[8] children were given the task of 'making friends' with a child who was a stranger to them, a task which the researchers subdivided into:

● Greeting (saying hi or hello).
● Asking the other child for some information about himself (e.g. what are your hobbies?).
● Including the child by inviting him to join a game (e.g. would you like to play marbles?).
● Telling the child something about yourself (e.g. I like playing Sindys).

Popular children were found to be much more adept at this sort of sequence than unpopular children. They knew how to say the right thing at the right time.

Unpopular children appear to be less aware of what is the right thing to say, or – more important – they may say the right thing at the wrong time. This was illustrated in a recent study by Ladd and Oden[9] in which children were shown cartoons depicting someone being teased or not understanding his school work and were asked what they thought would be the best thing to do to help in that situation. Most children varied their strategy according to the situation – they might, for example, console or comfort the 'friend' when they were alone together, but rarely when other children were watching. The less popular children, say the authors, were less aware of peer values and norms, less able to match their helping strategy appropriately to the situation.

So far we have looked at research with pre-school and primary-school children and identified 'rewardingness' and 'social knowledge' as possible factors contributing to popularity. With teenagers, qualities of cheerfulness, friendliness, enjoying jokes, having ideas for things to do, and good looks are all associated with being liked.[10] Being good at sport helps a boy to be popular but does not matter so much for girls. Unpopularity in teenagers of both sexes is associated with being restless, over-talkative and physically unattractive.

These findings highlight another important aspect of popularity, that of 'being different'. Research supports the widely held stereotype of the rejected child as an outsider, whether by looks, skin colour, physical handicap, or even such things as having an unusual name.[11] We choose our friends largely on the basis of perceived similarity to ourselves: the child who is different is always at a disadvantage.

Finally, popularity appears to be associated with certain parenting styles and with the quality of parent–child relationships. There is evidence that the child who gets off to a good start with a warm, secure relationship with his mother or other primary caregiver in his earliest years is more sociable and popular with his peers later on than the child who has a more ambivalent, anxious early attachment pattern.[12] Something that some parents do when the child is very small (psychologists have not yet got far in identifying the 'something', other than saying it means being responsive and sensitive to the child's signals) lays a foundation of social skill that helps him make and keep friends when he is older. Some things parents do when the child is of school age are also associated with popularity (though they do not necessarily cause it); mothers and fathers of likeable children have been found to discourage aggression, to make little use of physical punishment themselves, feel satisfied with their children and to show warmth and affection towards them.[13]

The lonely child: how to help

How to help a friendless child will depend on the reasons for his social isolation: there are different kinds of loneliness, and each calls for a different response. We can diagram some of these kinds like this:

THE LONELY CHILD

The unpopular or rejected child
Nominated by peers in answer to the question 'Who do you *not* like to play with?' Puts others off by his behaviour. May be restless and hyperactive, aggressive, boastful, attention-seeking, dominating. Is more likely than other children to develop emotional and behavioural problems later on in his life, possibly as a result of his early experiences of peer rejection.

The isolate Not actively rejected by his peers (i.e. not nominated as a person they dislike) but not positively chosen as a friend; receives no, or very few, choices on 'Who do you most like to play with?' No association with emotional problems later in life. No evidence that childhood isolates have subsequent adult difficulties. Tend to play on their own, but are not aggressive.

Prefers his own company: low in sociability – a trait he may have inherited from a parent

Lacks experience and know-how in approaching and playing with other children.

Is generally anxious and inhibited in new situations.

As we can see, there are two broad groups among the friendless, and one is more at risk of long-term outcome than the other.[14] Some children in the isolate, as opposed to the rejected, group may neither want nor need any help at all; whether by inherited temperament or the learned experience of playing contentedly alone, they have a lesser need of company than most children, and they like it that way. Others do want to make more friends, but don't know how to go about it or are afraid to try. For these children, the parent might consider:

● Using attention and other social rewards to encourage the child to play more with others. Like any other type of behaviour, sociable play is subject to learning and to the effects of positive consequences. In one very interesting experiment[15] which illustrates the effect of such consequences, a group of teachers tried to get boys and girls in a nursery school to play more with each other, rather than in all-girl or all-boy groups. When they saw a boy and girl playing together, they would go up and talk to them, perhaps commenting 'That's a nice game, you two.' The amount of mixed play *doubled* as a result of this strategy. Many individual shy children in nursery schools have been taught to be more sociable by a similar manipulation of adult attention. Very often, in ordinary life, nursery teachers or playgroup leaders go up to a child and talk to him when he is on his own; it has been found to work better if they reverse their normal pattern. Sometimes they need to shape social play by giving the child attention at first when he just watches others play, later only if he speaks to them, later still only if he joins in. Parents of shy children would have to look harder for opportunities to help in this way than would the teacher, but opportunities can still be found, in parks and playgroups and when the child is visiting or being visited. The idea is to avoid making it too interesting for the child to stay close to you in social situations, and to show him you approve when he does make a move towards other children. For example, when settling him into playgroup you will be there, in a particular spot where he can easily find you, for a few sessions – but you will be reading your own book or magazine and not wanting to read to him or do the puzzle he brings over to you. It will not be altogether easy to give him attention while he *is* playing with another child without the risk of distracting him, but there might be an opportunity to smile and say 'That looks fun' and, later on when you are both on your way home, to tell him how much you liked to see him on the slide with John, in the playhouse with all the others, or whatever.

● Engineering more opportunities for the child to play with others. This is the first thing most parents will think of if their child lacks friends, and there is no doubt that children whose parents have deliberately arranged more social contacts for them do have an advantage when it comes to friendship skills. Studies have shown, for example, that toddlers who had been taken to mother-and-toddler groups and visited/been visited by many children, played more often and for longer with others when observed by the research team than did toddlers who had not had such opportunities.[16] There is no substitute for direct experience in learning how to get on with others. Particularly important is regular contact with one 'special' playmate; it takes time for children to learn what games they both enjoy, and to be able to predict each other's behaviour well enough for smooth reciprocal social interaction; they need to be given the chance, over weeks and months, to get to know each other really well. Parents who arrange regular mutual visits and swaps for their children, from the toddler stage until the child is old enough to arrange his own, will be providing the right opportunities for this sort of friendship. More and more children today live in situations where they cannot safely or easily go out of their back doors and find someone to play with. Increasingly parents have to make artificial arrangements to replace this loss. If their child lacks a friend, they should not feel they are interfering or intruding if they go out and find one for him.

- Teaching the child how to go about approaching others or breaking into a group. This is different from the kind of anxious *general* encouragement ('Why don't you go and play with the others?') which is often given, but which may only increase the child's resistance. Instead the parent makes specific suggestions, based on knowledge of how children at various stages do go about making friends. Toddlers, for example, usually begin by offering each other toys; the parent can say 'Why don't you show that to –?' when the child is holding something attractive. With a group of slightly older pre-school children, the tactics change; again we need to know what children of this age actually do in social situations. It would *not* be helpful to suggest 'Why don't you go and ask Mary and Ruth if you can play too?' – the usual answer, it appears, would be 'No, you can't!' Observations[17] have shown that a three- or four-year-old who wants to join in a game will go and stand near the game and watch for a while, then 'encircle' the area he wants to play in, before entering the area and starting to do what the others are doing, alongside but not necessarily with them. The parent, then, seeing the child hanging around a pair who are building a tower with bricks, and obviously longing to join in, might suggest the child find his own box of bricks and play with them next to James and David. Older children are more direct in their approaches; as we saw earlier they might go up to someone they did not know, say hello, ask him something about himself and invite him to join in a particular game. Parents can rehearse this sequence with their shy child, parent and child each taking a part, then changing roles: in practice this is not nearly so difficult as it sounds.

- Avoiding using labels which the child might incorporate into his picture of himself and try to live up to. If he refuses to say hello to a strange adult or child you introduce him to, ignore it rather than make the excuse that he is shy. A child who hears, over and over again, that he is shy (or a bit of a baby, or a mummy's boy, or not very good with people) is likely to go on being all these things.

Approaches like these are meant for the child who is often or always on his own, but not actively rejected by his peers. The child who is disliked, and really unpopular, needs a different kind of help. Most commonly he needs to be induced, on the lines described in chapter 12, to be less aggressive in his dealings with others. Often his parents are the *only* people who can help him really effectively in this. They can, too, try to teach him the positive social skills which make for popularity: skills which we will now look at in detail.

Teaching social skills: problem solving

Two well-known American psychologists, Myrna Shure and George Spivack, believe and to some extent have demonstrated that social skills depend very much on how good a child is at thinking up many different ways of handling problems between people, and at evaluating the possible outcomes of each 'solution' to a problem. They feel that children can be taught to think more creatively about what to do in conflict situations; to this end they have devised programmes for use in schools, and by parents in the home,[18] which employ stories and puppets and make-believe games to teach better problem-solving techniques. In a typical 'lesson' given by a parent, for example, the child is shown a picture of two children playing with toys and asked to pretend he is one of those children wanting the other to help put the toys away. What, the parent asks, could he do so that the other boy would help him? The child thinks of all the things he might say or do, and the parent writes them down. He does not say one idea (like hitting the other boy) was a bad one, or another (like sharing some gum with the other boy if he helps) was a good one. He simply writes all the ideas down, saying things like 'Now we have two ideas . . . can you think of any more . . . what might X do? . . . what might Y feel? That's way number three.' Later in the series of lessons the child is asked 'What might happen next . . .?' so that he thinks about consequences for each of his proposed solutions and decides which one would be best. The final step is for the parents to use what Spivack and Shure call problem-solving dialogues in real-life situations, as part of their everyday way of talking with their child.

For an occasion, for example, when the child comes to a parent and says 'They won't play with me', Spivack and Shure describe the following dialogue:[18]

> *Child:* Robbie and Derek won't let me play.
> *Mother:* What are they doing?
> *Child:* They're cowboys. They chased me away.
> *Mother:* Do you want to play their game?
> *Child:* Yeah.
> *Mother:* What did you say to them?
> *Child:* I'm a cowboy too.

Mother: Then what happened?
Child: Derek said you're too little. You can't play.
Mother: What did you do then?
Child: Nothing.
Mother: Can you think of something different you can do or say so they
will let you play?
Child: I can say I'm a big cowboy.
Mother: What might happen if you do that?
Child: They'd say no, you're not.
Mother: They might say that. What else can you say or do?
Child: I could tell them Indians are coming. I could help catch them.
Mother: That's a different idea. Try your ideas and see what happens.

The parent in this situation could have intervened directly, asking Robbie
and Derek to let the younger child join in. He or she could have suggested
the younger child leave the others alone, and find a game he could play by
himself, or offered him a ready-made solution ('Why don't you get out a gun
each for them and one for you?'). Spivack and Shure argue that by *not* doing
any of these things, the parent is helping the child to develop his own
resources for solving problems.

Again, in the very common situation where two children want the same
toy, a problem-solving dialogue might go something like this:

Parent: What happened?
Child: Ben hit me.
Parent: Why did he hit you?
Child: I want to ride the bike now. He had a long turn.
Parent: So what did you do? What did you say?
Child: I got the bike.
Parent: How did Ben feel about that?
Child: Angry. He *hit* me.
Parent: How did you feel?
Child: Angry.
Parent: So, you're cross and Ben's cross and he hit you. Can you think of
any different ways of getting the bike so he won't be cross and hit you?
Child: I could tell you.
Parent: That's one idea. Can you think of any more?
Child: I could say I'd give it back straight away.
Parent: That's another one. Any more?
Child: I could tie a rope on and let him pull me like we did at his house.
Parent: What might happen if you told me?
Child: You'd say you're not interested in hearing about quarrels.
Parent: And if you said you'd give it straight back?
Child: He might not believe me.
Parent: And if you do the rope thing?
Child: He might . . . I'll try.

Causes, feelings, solutions and consequences: these are the four essential ideas of problem-solving. They are ideas which any parent can hold in his mind as a way of structuring a conversation with a child when things have gone wrong for him and his friends. They could be a very useful way of 'reasoning' with a child – for the talk part of the act-now-talk-later model of good parenting which is suggested by psychological research. These dialogues are a little different from the way we usually talk to children: they ask the child to think for himself rather than telling him what he should have done. Many parents might want to combine such dialogues, at least in the beginning, with supplying their own suggestions (for example, in the bicycle situation: 'You could each have five minutes') after the child has offered his. Either way, the two important questions, 'What else could you have done?' and 'What might have happened then?', are well worth asking children, and their answers are well worth listening to.

Teaching social skills: the art of being nice

Being nice to other people, doing as you would be done by: these are, research suggests, the key elements of popularity in childhood (and beyond). But they are vague goals for any child to aim at; it is more useful to break 'being nice' into its component sub-skills. Such an analysis might go like this:[19]

- Making positive remarks, offering compliments. Commenting on other people's strengths rather than their weaknesses. Not calling people names.
- Knowing how to make a request politely and persuasively: 'if you don't mind', 'If it wouldn't be too much trouble could you . . .' Saying 'please', and 'thank you'.
- Knowing how to apologize and receive apologies.
- Including someone who is left out . . . helping someone who needs help.
- Sharing and taking turns.
- Not cheating in games; being a good winner and a good loser.

Any parent looking at this list will be aware that he or she has been actively teaching some of these skills already, for much of the child's life, in particular those skills to do with taking turns, sharing and saying 'please', 'thank you' and 'sorry'. Rather fewer parents, however, will have had conversations like these with their children:

> *Child:* Move, Joanna!
> *Parent:* She's in your way, but there's a better way of asking. Try 'Would you mind moving over a little bit, Joanna, so that I can sit down.'

Parent: Suppose you'd just lost a game of cards. What could someone say that would make you feel better?

Child: Well . . . if he said something like 'I was lucky there . . . you played well though.'

Parent: Could you try saying that to Ian if you win the next game?

Parent: I'm going to pretend I'm Rob [the child's friend] coming up to you and saying 'Hey, I'm in the soccer team next Saturday. You didn't make it, did you?' Now I know you'd probably really tell me to get lost, but what else *could* you say. Just pretend.

Child: I'd say, I don't like football anyway.

Parent: Is that really how you'd feel?

Child: No. I would mind.

Parent: Why not say so – say what you feel?

Child: Then . . . I really wanted to be picked.

Parent: Can you say something nice to him, too? Remember he's feeling really pleased about it. What about something like 'I think it's great you did so well. I really wish I'd been picked too.'

In these exchanges the parent has done what all social skills training is all about; he has modelled what the child might do, and got him to try it out. It is not so elaborate as the training that might go on in schools or other social settings, where video demonstrations and role playing games are often used, but it is nevertheless effective.

There are several ways in which a parent might create opportunities for such exchanges:

● Intervening directly between the child and his brother/sister/friend, to model what he might say or do – 'John seems to be very sorry he knocked over your tower. What could you say? Why not tell him "That's OK?"' . . . 'Look, Jane can't do up her zip; perhaps you could help her' . . . 'You won, did you? and John said "Well done"? What should you say to him? I'd say "Thanks", and ask if he wanted another game' . . . 'Do you like the picture Mary did? Why don't you tell her so?' . . . and so on.

● Choosing one of the skills of 'being nice' and having the whole family practise that skill for a week: paying compliments to each other one week, making requests beginning 'Would you please . . .?' or 'Do you mind if . . .' the second week, not interrupting one another in conversation a third week.

● Playing a family game in which each person pulls out a card describing a social situation and has to say (or act out) what he would do in that situation. Examples might be:

Somebody says they think you are very good looking. What do you say?

Your set of coloured pencils is missing a purple; you want to borrow someone else's. How do you go about it?

You and some friends go ice skating. One of you keeps falling down. What do you do/say?

Someone at school writes a poem that is better than yours. What would you do/say?

Teaching social skills: being assertive

Just as important as teaching a child how to act in ways that will please others is to teach him to express his *own* needs, opinions and feelings – and to say 'no' where no is necessary. Assertiveness involves:

- Being able to express one's own opinion even if it differs from that of peers, parents or teachers.
- Being able to ask for help if you need it.
- Being able to complain if you have cause for complaint.
- Being able to make a suggestion about a game or activity; instructing someone else in what to do.
- Being able to refuse unreasonable requests.
- Being able to resist pressure from peers to do something you don't want to do or don't think is right.

Several researchers have tried, with some success, to teach children these skills. In one particularly interesting study, which has much to offer parents, Melinda Combs and Diana Slaby[20] had nursery school teachers model for the children what they might say in conflict situations, and to praise them for being appropriately assertive. These authors point out that few young children know how to react if another child hits them, barges in on their play or snatches a toy from them. Most either give in, or cry, or hit back, or go and tell the teacher. Nor do they know how to ask another child for something they want, or how to ask for help, and this is why they so often just grab or give up. In Combs and Slaby's study the teacher would say to a child, for example, 'You can *ask* for that', if he was trying to take another child's toy. He would be praised for asking, and for accepting the situation if the other child said 'no'. All the children were taught that they could and should say 'no' sometimes, but that there were special ways of saying 'no' that wouldn't make the other person cross: 'I'm playing with this now, but you can have it when I've finished.' Scenes were acted out for the children with a doll or puppet: the doll would 'hit' the child and the teacher would model what he should say – 'No hitting!' – in place of either hitting back or submitting. Other situations included saying 'Please don't lean on me, I don't like that' instead of pushing, 'No, I want to do it my way' instead of automatically giving in to what the doll wanted him to do, and asking for help in an ordinary non-whining tone of voice. All the children, even those as young as three, enjoyed this kind of play-acting and were later seen to make good use of the new skills they had learned.

Assertiveness is not just a matter of what a person says; most important is the *way* in which he says it. Research[21] has shown that successful assertiveness involves making direct eye contact, speaking fairly loudly and with emphasis, and standing upright with chest out, shoulders squared and hands perhaps on the hips. The simplest way to get this across to a child is to show him: the parent needs to try out how he or she would say 'NO HITTING!' and then have the child try it out too.

As with teaching the art of being nice, teaching the art of being assertive can mean direct intervention/demonstration while the child is playing with siblings or friends, or family discussion on the lines of 'What should you do if . . .' This is an example of direct intervention in one family:

> Linda and Paula were sisters, aged seven and five. Like many big sisters, Linda was quite bossy, and quite good at getting Paula to do what she wanted. One day when the girls were playing downstairs Linda asked Paula to go and fetch some pillows from upstairs for their acrobatics game. The girls' mother said 'You don't *have* to do what Linda says, you know. You can say "no".' This idea seemed never to have occurred to Paula; she was surprised but did manage to refuse Linda's request. After that she would often check with her mother: 'You said it was all right to say "no". I don't have to, do I?' and began to try out ways of standing up for her own rights.

The second kind of teaching, family discussion about being assertive, could begin from imagined situations like these:

> You're watching television with some others; one of them keeps on talking so you can't hear the programme. What do you do?

> You lent your new rubber to a friend and it comes back in two pieces. What would you do?

> Imagine your teacher had promised you first turn with the computer one day at school but, when you get to it, you find someone else already there. What do you do?

> A friend gives you the money to buy her a lipstick when you go into town. You can't get the one she wanted so you buy a different brand. She says it's the wrong colour. What do you do?

> The others want you to join in playing a joke on the teacher; you don't want to. What do you do?

> The heel comes off a pair of shoes you bought a week ago. What should you do?

> You're in a group planning a school project and you have a good idea.
> You start to explain it when someone interrupts. What will you do?

One way of helping children to think about how to be assertive without also being negative and aggressive comes from questions which make them put themselves in another's place: if someone did not agree with you/did not like what you did/were angry with you, how would you want him to tell you?[22] Thinking about these questions, children will usually answer that they want the other person to state clearly and calmly how he feels, without calling them names or yelling at them. 'I feel really mad you told on me', 'I don't think X, I think Y', 'I don't like it when you . . .'. They can use these as models for their own assertive behaviour, when they meet a situation which calls for assertiveness.

Teaching social skills: coping with teasing and bullying

Looking back on our own childhood, many of us have vivid and unhappy memories of being teased or bullied or put under pressure by peers. Yet we have probably very few memories of telling our parents about any of this, or talking it over with them. The world of a child and his peers is often intensely private. Many children put up with the miseries of, for example, bullying, without ever thinking what else they might be able to do about the situation. For this reason, it is particularly important that family conversations about 'What you would do if . . .' do take place, preferably before the child meets the situation in real life. In conversations like these, a variety of solutions to interpersonal conflict can be put forward and evaluated. Many children, when talking about a situation in which *someone else* is being bullied or picked on, would see that they should not just stand by in silent collusion, and that 'telling' might be the most adult and responsible thing to do. They might then be more able to let a trusted teacher know if they themselves were at the receiving end of bullying. Many children also need to talk about teasing; we may not be able to give them one right way of handling it, but we can help them come up with several alternatives, and guide them to a realization that retaliation – though the most common reaction to teasing – is in most circumstances the least effective response.

> You get called a swot because the teacher liked your work. What would be best?
>
> ● Being assertive – saying 'I did good work and I'm happy about that.'
> ● Understanding the other person's feelings – 'Not much fun watching someone else get all the praise, I know.'
> ● Avoiding – you walk away and ignore them, or you change the subject.
> ● Retaliating – 'Just 'cos *you're* so stupid . . .'

Two boys keep following you home from school and calling out names. What should you try?

- Being assertive – saying 'When you call me names I feel very angry. I'm telling you, now, to stop.'
- Retaliating – getting into a fight.
- Avoiding – going into the nearest shop, library or wherever, and staying there until they get bored and give up.

A girl calls you names because you are going out with her ex-boyfriend, whom she still likes. What should you try?

- Being assertive – 'I don't like the names you are calling me, and I want it to stop. I think we could both try to find a way to be friends again,'
- Avoiding – ignore her.
- Retaliating – tell her you can see why the boyfriend gave her up.
- Understanding her feelings – 'Listen, I should probably feel the same if this happened to me . . . I know it really hurts. Let's talk about it.'

Teaching social skills: self-control

For some children – often the least popular ones – the kind of self-control needed to handle conflict constructively is very hard to achieve. If teased, criticized or provoked in any way, they tend to lash out, without stopping to think and consider alternatives. It may be helpful to teach a child like this some very specific techniques developed by teachers and psychologists to slow down their impulsive reactions and encourage better conflict resolution:

- Negotiation skills.[23] The parent can best teach these in a situation where he and the child disagree. The parent states his position and his feelings (e.g. 'I want you to keep your room tidy. When I see your things all over the floor I feel angry') and asks the child to state his ('I am happy with my room as it is. I think it's my room so I should be able to do what I like with it'). The parent models *listening* to this opinion, in an open way, trying to understand how the child feels. He restates what he believes to be the child's position so as to get things clear. He then suggests a compromise ('Perhaps if I didn't go into your room, I wouldn't feel angry. How about if you take the responsibility for cleaning the room and changing the sheets?'). The three-step model of handling conflict is discussed: first each of you says what he thinks; then you listen openly to what the other person thinks and try to guess what he is feeling; then you suggest a compromise. The child is encouraged to use this strategy when he next finds himself disagreeing with a friend, teacher or parent.
- The boiling point list.[24] The child sits down with an adult and generates a list of situations which make him angry (being told off at school, being

called names, etc.); he then rates each situation on a one-to-five scale according to whether it just bothers him a little, or makes him really mad. This procedure will help him become more aware of the danger situations where he will most need to exercise self-control.

- The turtle technique.[25] Really just a variant of the old count-to-ten method, this is a simple technique children can be taught to use when they feel themselves becoming angry or upset. It makes use of the analogy of a turtle, who when it is threatened withdraws into its shell rather than 'sticking its neck out'. The child is shown how to pull both his arms and head in close to his body, imagining himself safe inside his shell; he breathes deeply and lets all his muscles go loose, giving himself time to think of all the possible ways he might handle the situation.
- The circle game.[26] The child stands in the centre of a group while the others tease and try to provoke him. He has to say to himself 'I will not get angry', 'I will not fight'. Then it is his turn to be on the outside of the circle.

Social skills: who should be the teacher?

All of these examples are things a parent *can* teach his child to help him develop better social skills. It is not, however, as easy for parents as it might be: they will usually find themselves at one remove from the real-life conflicts the child may be facing, talking in terms of the hypothetical rather than the actual. After the child is five or so, it is never so easy to teach social skills as it was when opportunities presented themselves daily around sandpit, or playhouse, or swing. As the child grows older, his parents spend less and less time with him in a group. The people who are best placed to teach social skills are those who *do* deal with children in social settings. It is in such settings that, ideally, topics like bullying and teasing and group pressure should be discussed, and in such settings that children and teenagers can try out alternative ways of behaving. Increasingly, videotapes and packaged discussion materials on such topics are becoming available to teachers and school counsellors; social skills may one day be part of every child's school curriculum. But for the moment, in the most part, if social skills training is done at all, it is done at home, and parents will need to think about introducing 'What would you do if . . .?' conversations into their children's lives at least once in a while.

References

1 M. B. Parten, 'Social play among school children', *J. Abn. Soc. Psychol.*, 28 (1932), 136–47.
2 J. Rubenstein and C. Howes, 'The effects of peers on toddler interaction with mother and toys', *Child Dev.*, 47 (1976), 597–605.

3 P. K. Smith, 'Social and fantasy play in young children', in B. Tizard and D. Harvey (eds), *Biology of Play*, London, Heinemann, 1977.

4 Z. Rubin, *Children's Friendships*, London, Open Books Publishing/Fontana, 1980.

5 L. C. Lee, 'Social encounters of infants: the beginnings of popularity', paper presented at the biennial meetings of the International Society for the Study of Behavioural Development, Ann Arbor, Michigan, 1973.

6 W. Hartup, J. Glazer and R. Charlesworth, 'Peer reinforcement and sociometric status', *Child Dev.*, 38 (1967), 1017–24.

7 S. Oden and S. R. Asher, 'Coaching children in social skills for friendship making', *Child Dev.*, 48 (1977), 495–506.

8 J. Gottman, J. Gonso and B. Rasmussen, 'Social interaction, social competence and friendship in children', *Child Dev.*, 46 (1975), 709–18.

9 G. W. Ladd and S. Oden, 'The relationship between peer acceptance and children's ideas about helpfulness', *Child Dev.*, 50 (1979), 402–8.

10 J. Coleman, *The Nature of Adolescence*, London, Routledge and Kegan Paul, 1980.

11 S. Oden, 'A child's social isolation: origins, prevention, intervention', in G. Cartledge and J. F. Milburn, *Teaching Social Skills to Children: Innovative Approaches*, New York, Pergamon, 1980.

12 E. Waters, J. Wippman and L. A. Sroufe, 'Attachment, positive affect and competence in the peer group: two studies in construct validation', *Child Dev.*, 50 (1979), 821–9.

13 W. Hartup, 'Peer relations and family relations: two social worlds', in M. Rutter (ed.), *Scientific Foundations of Developmental Psychiatry*, London, Heinemann Medical Books, 1980.

14 K. Tiffen and S. Spence, 'Responsiveness of isolated versus rejected children to social skills training', *J. Child Psychol. Psychiatry*, 27 (1986), 343–55.

15 L. A. Serbin, J. J. Tonick and S. H. Sternglanz, 'Shaping cooperative cross-sex play', *Child Dev.*, 48 (1977), 924–9.

16 E. Mueller and J. Brenner, 'The origins of social skill and interaction among playgroup toddlers', *Child Dev.*, 48 (1977), 854–61.

17 W. A. Corsara, 'We're friends, right? Children's use of access rituals in a nursery school', *Language in Society*, 8 (1979), 315–36.

18 M. Shure and G. Spivack, *Problem Solving Techniques in Child-Rearing*, San Francisco, Jossey-Bass, 1978.

19 M. Sapon-Shevin, 'Teaching cooperation in early childhood settings', in G. Cartledge and J. F. Milburn (eds), *Teaching Social Skills to Children: Innovative Approaches*, New York, Pergamon, 1980.

20 M. Combs and D. A. Slaby, 'Social skills training with children', *Advances in Clinical Child Psychology*, vol. 1, New York, Plenum Press, 1977.

21 M. Argyle, *The Psychology of Interpersonal Behaviour*, 4th edn., Harmondsworth, Penguin, 1983.

22 S. A. Fagan, N. J. Long and D. J. Stevens, *Teaching Children Self-Control*, Columbus, Ohio, Charles E. Merrill, 1975.

23 A. P. Goldstein, R. P. Sprafkin, N. J. Gershaw and P. Klein, 'The adolescent: social skills training through structured learning', in G. Cartledge and J. F. Milburn (eds), *Teaching Social Skills to Children: Innovative Approaches*, New York, Pergamon, 1980.

24 R. L. Curwin and G. Curwin, *Developing Individual Values in the Classroom*, Palo Alto, Education Today, 1974.
25 M. Schneider and A. Robin, 'The turtle technique: a method for self-control of impulse behaviour', unpublished manuscript, State University of New York at Stony Brook, 1975.
26 S. E. Goodwin and M. J. Mahoney, 'Modification of aggression through modelling: an experimental probe', *J. Behav. Therapy and Experimental Psychiatry*, 6 (1975), 200–02.

16 Overview

It would be a superhuman parent who adopted all, or even half of the ideas in this book. Many readers will feel that the roles they are asked here to play – roles of teacher, counsellor, behaviour therapist – are too many and too complex for the ordinary person to take on. Bringing up children, they will say (and quite rightly too) is hard work: it is difficult enough sometimes to keep track of their socks, never mind their social skills. Parents, moreover, have other things to do than just bring up their children, and other things on their minds. They have jobs, problems, relationships: good days and bad days. A large part of everyday parenting has to do with what the parent/him or herself is feeling; when we shout at children, or nag, or smack, or criticize, it is often because of our own psychological 'needs' at that moment rather than because we necessarily believe that what we are doing is right for the child. We express, as parents, our own wants and needs and personality in our relationships with our children, and we always will.

Nevertheless, if we can't be ideal parents all of the time, we still need a sense of what we ought to be doing, and of how – on a good day, in the right conditions, if we weren't so busy – we would like to be bringing up our children. It is here that psychological knowledge can be uniquely helpful, in the sense that it allows us to base the 'ought' not on the way we ourselves were brought up, or on what mother-in-law says, or on whatever may be the currently fashionable ethos (veering over the years from permissive to authoritarian and back again), but on something a little more solid.

The important parts

What, then, are the important parts in all this? What do all these psychological studies of children and their families really have to say to parents? What themes, if any, run through research on parenting styles and methods of discipline, on communication and common childhood problems?

● First, the research reviewed here suggests that we should not, as parents, be afraid to be *in charge* in our dealings with children. Children need guidelines for their behaviour, and they need these guidelines to be firmly and consistently upheld. It is possible to be authoritative without being a tyrant; we should always listen to children, but we should not expect them to have a wisdom and good sense that is greater than our own.

● Children manipulate parents as much as parents control children – though neither may be aware of it. To understand what is going on between a parent and a child, we need to look at the positive and negative consequences each is applying to the behaviour of the other. To change behaviour, we need to alter those consequences. Reward systems and alternatives to punishment, like time out and logical consequences, are based on this principle and are practical and effective as tools for improving parent–child relationships.

● Tools like these are best applied to the immediate situation, to resolve an immediate problem. But they need to be followed up later on with discussion. We can adopt a strategy of 'act now – talk later', but we *should* find the time (more than we do at present) to talk: about problems between people, about how each person feels in a given situation, about possible alternative solutions and alternative outcomes.

● Listening to and restating the feelings behind words is a skill any parent can learn, and one which will enable him or her to communicate more effectively within the family.

● Parents can help their children with everyday behaviour problems, fears and worries; they are in a much better position to help than any outsider. There is no need to feel helpless in the face of a child who won't do as she's told, or wets her bed at the age of nine, or can't seem to stop sucking her thumb, or argues incessantly with her sister, or won't go to school: these are problems that can be solved.

Seeking help

If the ideas from books like this *don't* seem to be solving a problem, the next step for parents might be to seek outside help. The professionals they meet in the helping agencies will be unlikely, however, to tackle the problem in ways that are radically different from those which parents – aware of current psychological ideas – might have tried already. What they can do is help a family put those ideas into practice in a consistent, organized way. What they can also do is enable families to think through a problem calmly and productively with someone who is not quite so close to it or so emotionally involved, and encourage family members to find new ways of communicating with each other. The professionals will not on the whole try to solve problems by working directly with the child; they too realize that the best people to help are the child's own family, and see their job in terms of making this possible.

Some of the types of problems with which parents might well need outside help were discussed in chapter 8: serious depression in children, anxieties or obsessions which are affecting them to the extent of interfering with their daily lives, some kinds of stealing or aggressive, antisocial behaviour, profound alienation of an adolescent from his or her family, specific disorders such as anorexia, bedwetting or soiling, and more general long-term problems like an inability to make and keep friends. Most professionals, however, would also be more than willing to spend time with parents working out joint solutions to less serious problems too: they know that a little help at an early stage is often more useful than a lot of help later on, and their experience of similar problems in other families can offer valuable short-cuts in the path to change.

Such professionals – who might be child psychiatrists, clinical or educational psychologists, or social workers – can be found working in settings which vary from area to area: the district health authority will have information about hospital and child and family guidance clinics in their locality, the local education authority about its own psychological services, and the social services department about family centres and other facilities which they can offer.

The future

Research on parenting is changing. Once it was a matter of having parents fill in questionnaires about their attitudes to child-rearing, and trying to find relationships between these broad attitudes and the personality and adjustment of the children. Now research is more concerned with specifics, with the details of what parents and children actually *do* in each other's company: psychologists are counting the number of times a parent touches a child in an hour, or the percentage of play episodes between mother and baby that the older sibling joins in, or the proportion of a mother's instructions which she follows and the proportion she ignores. It may all seem, to parents themselves, somewhat suspect – a bit of pseudo-science. But it is leading to a better understanding of many important issues; it is on occasion producing some surprising findings – findings that are more than just a restatement of ordinary common sense, like those of the Cambridge group on the origins of jealousy between siblings. The painstaking, detailed observations that lead to such findings are the direction which psychological research on parenting will increasingly take in the future.

Many questions remain to be addressed by research. We need to know more about the long-term effectiveness of problem-solving dialogues and social-skill teaching. We need to develop and evaluate ways of helping children to gain a feeling of mastery over their environment, and a certainty that they can cope with stress if it comes. We need to know more about how to foster appropriate assertiveness without its tipping over into aggression. We need to resolve the contradictory notions that going to your infant straight away whenever she cries will on the one hand help her develop a sense that her needs will be reliably met and a secure attachment, and, on the other hand, teach her in the long term to cry and fuss more and to be more difficult. We need to know how we can foster the 'sensitive' caretaking in the child's earliest months and years, which research has shown to be linked with secure attachment and later emotional adjustment. We need to know much more about the part played by fathers in the child's world and about parenting as it moves away from the traditional model of the nuclear family and takes on new and varied forms.

Many of these questions will one day be answered; some are on the way to being answered already. Whether we will ever get to the real crux of the matter of being a parent is less certain. We do not yet really understand, and perhaps never will understand, what it is that makes the parent care so much about his or her child, and the child know that she is loved and valued; yet this is the foundation for all that is good in their relationship, and of the child's ability to cope confidently with life. In this sense, so long as much remains beyond the cold realms of observation, measurement and analysis, parenting will continue to be an art rather than a science – and perhaps that is, ultimately, how most of us would want it to stay.

Index

sex differences—*continued*
  in behaviour, 2
  sibling relationships and, 112
sexuality, 51, 52, 122
shaping, 23–4
shopping, 27, 44
Shure, M., 128, 129
shyness, 52–3, 66, 67, 125–8
siblings *see* brothers and sisters
Slaby, D., 132
sleep
  in parents' bed, 8, 9, 48
  problems, 3, 43, 44, 48, 49–50, 55, 111
  walking, 4, 50
smacking, 35–7, 38, 102, 104, 107
  see also physical punishment
sociability, 4, 125
social skills
  popularity and, 123–4
  problem-solving and, 128
  teaching of, 128–36
soiling, 32, 50–1, 141
Spivack, G., 128, 129
Spock, Dr, 9
stammering *see* stuttering
star charts, 27–9, 30, 89, 92, 97–8, 99, 105
stealing, 19, 53, 141
stress
  coping with, 59
  types of, 58–9
  problem behaviours and, 49, 50, 54–5
strictness, 9–11
stuttering, 4, 55
styles of parenting
  authoritarian, 10–11
  authoritative, 11–12, 140
  consistency in, 7
  overprotective, 7–8
  popularity and, 124–5
sucking habits, 96–8
sulking, 4
swearing, 39–40, 42

table manners, 30
tantrums, 4, 22, 42, 43–4, 45–6, 60
Taylor, E., 54
teachers
  attention of, as a reward, 19, 21, 26, 42, 43

learning from concrete experiences and, 74
school problems and, 31–2, 91, 134
social skills and, 136
teasing
  coping with, 134–5
  fears and, 86
  habits and, 97
teenagers *see* adolescence
television, 103, 119
temperament
  in infancy, 2
  individual differences in, 2–3, 49, 53, 59, 66, 84
  parental handling and, 2, 3, 102, 104
  sibling relationships and, 112
  sociability and, 125–6
temptation, resistance to, 10, 11, 36, 38, 40, 117
thinking
  abstract, 74
  egocentric, 70–1, 77
  in adolescence, 74
  in middle childhood, 74
  in young children, 69–74
  magical, 72
Thomas, A., 3, 102
threats, 14, 40, 47, 90, 104, 107
thumbsucking, 28, 39, 94, 96–8
tics, 55
tidying up, 27, 28, 31, 33, 47, 65, 135–6
time, 74, 77–8
time out, 44–6, 107, 118
timidity *see* anxiety, fears
tiredness, 44, 47, 53, 55, 104
toddlers, 20, 44, 60, 122, 126, 127
toilet training, 9, 32, 111
Tosti, D., 24
treats, 22, 28–9, 40
twin studies, 4

water, fear of, 86, 88
whining, 4, 22, 24, 42, 43–4
Winnicot, D., 95
Wolff, S., 53, 59, 60, 61
worries *see* anxiety, fears